Authority and the Liberal Tradition

Authority and the Liberal Tradition

A RE-EXAMINATION OF THE CULTURAL
ASSUMPTIONS OF AMERICAN LIBERALISM

Robert A. Heineman

Carolina Academic Press
Durham, North Carolina

To the memory of Cora and Helen

Library of Congress Catalog Card Number: 83–71825
International Standard Book Number: 0–89089–271–7 (cloth)
0–89089–272–5 (paper)

Carolina Academic Press
Post Office Box 8795, Forest Hills Station
Durham, North Carolina 27707

Designed by J. Webb
Printed in the United States of America

Contents

Contents

Preface

L iberal ideas have become so integral to American political thinking that they are simply assumed in most discussions of policy. Just as one does not carefully examine the door one opens daily to one's home or the chair at one's desk, so liberal assumptions have become a part of the cultural landscape that has eluded serious analysis. Unfortunately, unlike a broken chair or an ill-fitting door, the effects of ideas that have outlived their usefulness or are in need of adjustment are often not readily apparent to those who continue to be guided by them. When finally exposed to the light of analysis, unexamined political ideas may display contradictions and weaknesses that help to explain policies that have appeared ill considered or have proven ineffectual. Thus, in addition to the substantial intellectual pleasure that it can provide, examination of the origins and assumptions of a nation's dominant belief system may also have a salutary influence on the methods and goals of public policy.

It is my position that the American liberal ideological system no longer enables democratic government to achieve its full potential because the ideas in that system have become too diffuse and superficial to be useful guides to action. I am suggesting that a fresh look at the Anglo-American liberal intellectual tradition from the perspective of an important need of the current era, that of authoritative democratic government, may produce useful insights for the American public and their leaders in terms of both the formulation and implementation of policy. The conclusions to be drawn from this study will vary depending on the orientation of the reader. The goal is not to provide a particular substantive answer to today's political problems but to persuade the reader that democratic government can be and must be more than it is today and that understanding liberal thinkers from the perspective of the cultural assumptions and social conditions within which they wrote can be helpful in moving in this direction.

I have been encouraged and helped by far more individuals than would be reasonably possible to thank here, but some are especially salient at this time. George C. S. Benson has been throughout a friend and invaluable advisor. Indeed, all of the people from Claremont have been helpful and encouraging, particularly Henry Salvatori, who is a serious student of ideas and a dedicated benefactor to intellectuals. Steven Peterson and Thomas Leitko performed valuable collegial duty by reading and commenting on the entire manuscript. Roland Warren thoroughly read, critiqued, and discussed the manuscript with me and provided me with the advantage of the ideas of a scholar of a markedly different ideological perspective. All three of these individuals demonstrated how stimulating honest, intellectually rigorous interchange can be. Russell Kirk has been consistently encouraging and helpful and took the initiative to bring to the attention of others a paper of mine that was presented at the Southern Political Science Convention and that contained some of my early ideas on liberalism. Tareq Ismael as always has been a friend and confidant. Mavis Thompson and Ellen Baker have labored diligently both as typists and office managers to move this effort toward fruition, and the staff at Herrick Library have been consistently helpful. I would also like to thank Michael Lakin for helping me to improve my presentation of several important points. My family—Alice, Philip, Karen, and Cheryl —have striven successfully to provide a pleasant environment for thinking and writing. Finally, I thank the Salvatori Center at Claremont McKenna College for their support and hospitality and Alfred University for their cooperation in allowing me time and assistance to complete this work. I thoroughly enjoyed re-examining the liberal tradition and the foregoing people and institutions have been important contributors to this experience. None, however, bears any responsibility for the judgments rendered herein or any accompanying sins of omission or commission.

Introduction

The motivation for this investigation into Anglo-American liberal thought stems from the concern that contemporary American culture, a product of centuries of liberal ideas, is incapable of supporting for any sustained period of time a government that acts with firmness and coherent direction. In light of huge governmental expenditures and the pervasiveness of governmental regulation, it may seem nonsensical to assert that liberal ideology has issued in government lacking in authority and direction. In fact, however, the tremendous expansion of government within the past several decades does not chart a rise in public regard for political authority but instead reflects the degree to which government must turn to coercion and material inducement to achieve its ends. Furthermore, these ends are as diffuse and varied as the opinions coloring the social fabric, for the expansion of governmental activity is a direct consequence of the inability of public officials to withstand the demands made of them. Because the welfare liberal ideology dominant since the New Deal provides no conceptual resources for effective governmental direction, public officials are left hastening to satisfy the immediate wants of their politically articulate publics. Effective government must be able to exercise restraint as well as be able to act firmly and directively, and to this end its officials must possess sufficient authoritative status in the public mind to allow them the choice of rejecting the demands made of them. But today's government is little more than a dart board on which competing interests record their various scores. The result has been that contemporary American government is seriously limited in its capacity to act for the national good as defined by it.

American government has, of course, in a general fashion always been responsive to the needs of the public as expressed by the citizenry. But in the current era this sensitivity to public whims has led to a diffuseness of policy focus that has bordered on impotence during a period when crises engendered by such objective factors as resource scarcity, technological advance, and population growth have loomed larger and larger. Presently of threatening proportions, these forces will be overwhelming if American governments are not able to act more efficiently and imaginatively. In his *The Zero-Sum Society*, Lester Thurow declares that "fundamental problems, such as the energy crisis, exist but cannot be solved. We have lost the ability to get things done...."[1] Discussing the problems that Keynesian economic principles pose in American democracy, James Buchanan and Richard Wagner comment on the inability of American politicians to make hard decisions. "A nation cannot survive with political institutions that do not face up squarely to the essential fact of scarcity.... Scarcity is indeed a fact of life, and political institutions that do not confront this fact threaten the existence of a prosperous and free society."[2] Others have drawn into question the future of democracy in more graphic terms. In his *An Inquiry Into the Human Prospect*, Robert Heilbroner sees the problems posed by technological change, population growth, and the weakening of the human spirit in industrial nations as so serious that "passage through the gauntlet ahead may be possible only under governments capable of rallying obedience far more effectively than would be possible in a democratic setting. If the issue for mankind is survival, such governments may be unavoidable, even necessary...."[3] For Jonathan Schell, the issue is the survival of the human race, and he is clear that in the face of the dangers posed by nuclear weapons a fundamental re-examination of political ideas and institutions is required. In a comparison particularly appropriate to the evolution of liberal ideology, he argues that nations are utilizing "Newtonian politics" in an "Einsteinian world."[4] Although Schell appears to be pleading for one-world government, one obvious ramification of his position is that governments must be sufficiently powerful to rise above narrow emotionalism in order to be able to act on behalf of mankind. Something serious has obviously happened to the government whose Constitution was once described by Gladstone as the "most wonderful work ever struck off at a given time by the brain and purpose of man." Thinkers such as Heilbroner

---

[1] Lester C. Thurow, *The Zero-Sum Society* (New York: Basic Books, 1980), p. 24.

[2] James M. Buchanan and Richard E. Wagner, *Democracy in Deficit* (New York: Academic Press, 1977), p. 184.

[3] Robert Heilbroner, *An Inquiry Into the Human Prospect* (New York: W. W. Norton, 1974), p. 110. Other studies than those mentioned in the text have raised similar questions about the future of democratic government. See, for example, Michael J. Crozier, Samuel P. Huntington, and Joji Watanuki, *The Crisis of Democracy* (New York: New York University Press, 1975).

[4] Jonathan Schell, *The Fate of the Earth* (New York: Alfred A. Knopf, 1982), p. 188.

are calling for much more than simple reforms to improve the democratic system. They are questioning its ability to survive.

Inceptionally, American government at the national level operated within the confines of the Constitution, which provides for three branches of government and allots power to each of them. Today, however, much of the formalism and many of the powers contained in the Constitution have been undermined by the distinctly American phenomenon of sub-governments, which have increased in power and number with the proliferation of organized interest groups in society. These sub-governments develop from the policy relationships growing out of the needs of interest groups and their related executive agencies and congressional committees. Thus, for example, the House Agriculture Committee contains mostly congressmen from farming areas who are responsible to agricultural groups and who oversee the funding and activities of the Agriculture Department. It is to the mutual benefit of these three elements to work closely together in the formulation of agricultural policy and to resist efforts from outside forces, such as those represented by the presidency, to intervene in this limited policy area. The multiplication of these sub-government relationships at the national level has made it increasingly difficult for a President or a congressional majority to provide policy direction.

The importance of political interest groups in the policy process was ably chronicled as early as 1908 by Arthur Bentley in his *The Process of Government* and later by David Truman in his *The Governmental Process.*[5] But the applicability of the largely economic focuses of Bentley and Truman has now been brought into question by the appearance of important non-economic political interest groups also intent upon tying into the sub-government game. Where these interests have not yet been able to build close agency-congressional relationships, they have often been successful in using the courts to influence the policy process, and, although they are a fairly recent development, their political effectiveness has contributed significantly toward greater policy divisiveness at the national level.

The decade of the sixties saw the beginnings of the marked increase in groups intent on pursuing intangible, normative goals through sophisticated political techniques. Previous to this time, much of government's activity was in response to demands on its ability to distribute economic rewards and occasionally, as with Prohibition, on its power to prohibit a particular activity. The new reforming spirit is characterized by charismatic leaders who often utilize their followings to try to force govern-

---

[5] Arthur F. Bentley, *The Process of Government* (Evanston, IL.: Principia Press, 1949 [First Published in 1908]); David B. Truman, *The Governmental Process* (New York: Alfred A. Knopf, 1951).

ment to impose their particular valuational perspective on the rest of society. In this respect, the personal rewards to be derived from leading a cause should not be underestimated. The leitmotif of activist reform has been the emergence throughout the political grassroots of individuals whose dedication to a particular form of social justice has enabled escape from lives described by George Steiner as a "gray transit between domestic spasm and oblivion."[6] The influence of even small groups is magnified by elected officials' sensitivity to the incremental nature of the electoral process. They know that, especially in a close election, a dedicated, well-organized minority, whether it be the antivivisectionists or irate vegetarians, can bring them to grief. Unfortunately, many of these new interest groups have found it to their advantage to exploit and encourage cynicism toward governmental officials, a tactic that was aided by the actions of many officials from the Vietnam War period through the Nixon resignation. The results of this approach may be liberating to group power, but they have contributed heavily to weakening the status of governmental authority. This has been particularly apparent at the national level.

The effects of those interests questioning and opposing America's involvement in Vietnam, for example, remain important limiting influences on this nation's power in foreign policy. It should be obvious to most informed Americans and to observant foreign leaders that, due to the power of latent domestic interests, this nation, barring direct attack on itself, is incapable of maintaining any sustained military effort anywhere. In fact, this limitation was to an extent formalized shortly after the Vietnamese conflict in the enactment of the 1973 War Powers Act, which specifically forbids the President to commit troops beyond sixty days without congressional approval.[7] But even if Congress were to approve longer commitment of troops, it is inconceivable that the government could for long withstand the antiwar pressures that would be brought to bear by ideological groupings and anti-militarist interests. During the Vietnam conflict, while American troops were dying in the south, important American figures took it upon themselves to defy government policy and visit the homeland of the enemy in a highly publicized fashion. A parallel situation may develop in El Salvador, for today important public figures are raising funds to aid the insurgents while American troops are acting as advisors to the legal government there. In this instance, public fear of military involvement is so great that when an American advisor was seen carrying a rifle near a war zone, it was an

---

[6] George Steiner, *In Bluebeard's Castle* (New Haven: Yale University Press, 1971), p. 87.

[7] These provisions apply to combat situations and the President has an additional thirty days if troops cannot be safely removed at the end of the sixty-day period.

important news story and cause for congressional concern. Whatever one's position on the Vietnamese War and the conflict in El Salvador, it should be clear from the events surrounding these conflicts that the national government has been brought to heel by non-economic interests proficient at mobilizing public support and fear. Moreover, it should be obvious to foreign nations, including America's enemies, that, although this nation has important sanctions that it can apply internationally and probably has the most powerful military force in the world, in the final analysis it is too weak to be able to commit its troops effectively.

On another front, the interest-group politics involved in the Alaska pipeline provide a good example of the ability of the newer forms of group activity to complicate the formulation of coherent domestic policy. In 1968, the oil companies determined that the northern Alaska region had tremendous oil and gas reserves; by 1970, they were in the planning stages for extracting these resources. It should be noted that, in terms of chronology, the oil companies were acting with some foresight before the energy crisis became acute. Nonetheless, they could hardly have been prepared for the onslaught of delaying tactics that environmentalist groups unleashed against them. Turning to the courts and invoking every sort of procedural stalling tactic that they could command, the environmentalists were successful in delaying activity on the needed oil pipeline across Alaska for three years. They might still be obstructing the extraction of Prudhoe Bay oil if it were not for the Arab oil embargo of 1973. At that point, in an exceptionally rare maneuver, Congress cleared the way for the pipeline by simply prohibiting the filing of further environmental suits against it in Federal courts. Finally, in 1977, oil from the new oil fields flowed across Alaska. One can only speculate on the effects that the Alaskan oil might have had on the energy crisis if it could have been obtained earlier, but no one should mistake the political power of non-economic interests as demonstrated by this abbreviated case study. Despite the widespread belief that the nation was on the verge of a national emergency, there is little question that the environmentalists, without the highly unusual action by Congress, would have continued to block the production and shipment of new oil.

Much of government's current impotence can be attributed to the inability of public officials and the general public to adjust to the new political parameters created by the rise of non-economically driven interests. Traditional interest demands of government expected tangible rewards, and public officials could manipulate and redistribute the public largesse until an acceptable compromise was reached. But the recent arrivals to the political scramble expect something different. They want governmental enforcement of a wide range of values, each set of which is peculiar to a particular grouping. Compromise in terms of material disbursement is very often irrelevant to them and, in terms of ideology, impossible. Liberal thought today is of little assistance to public officials because, as conceived by thinkers such as John Dewey, it assumed the primacy of process and compromise. In Dewey's time, it was relatively simple to explain the political process in terms of economic interests trying to get their share, but it is now apparent that under contemporary conditions such a view is dangerously superficial, for it focuses on the epiphenomena of one era and avoids the question of the position of political authority *qua* political authority. Before American public officials can be expected to resolve, through democratic means, the ideological impasses that are threatening, they must be provided with a conceptual framework that justifies the integrity of political authority within a democratic system. Superficial democratic liberalism was viable as an ideological framework for policy formulation until recently because the focus on economic concerns operated on a base of social stability. The newer forms of interest-group activity have destroyed this social base, however, by articulating valuational positions that are fundamentally incompatible and insisting that these positions be dealt with politically. Thus, on the abortion issue, government is left trying to muddle from one policy problem to another as the pro-life forces and pro-choice forces attempt to interject their causes wherever possible.

The purpose of this examination of the Anglo-American liberal intellectual heritage is to show that these ideas owe a great deal to governmental and non-governmental forms of social control. The causes for the present ideological quagmire can be traced to fundamental misunderstanding on the part of contemporary Americans about the nature of Anglo-American liberalism and its relationship to the social conditions within which it developed. Liberalism has failed to meet the demands on the political system because its spokesmen have refused to acknowledge its debt to forces of social stability and thus have been unwilling to admit that governmental power in and of itself might be a social good. Unfortunately, the politicization of diverse social interests has destroyed the stable framework within which governmental officials could once act with some confidence and coherence and has left them floundering in a sea of aggressive and increasingly irreconcilable demands. Before it will be possible to persuade liberal thinkers to undertake a fundamental reconceptionalization of the sources and importance of political authority, they must first be convinced that liberalism and social control are not antithetical.

Authoritative government need not be authoritarian government. Liberalism, which has done so much to advance social improvement, economic prosperity, and individual freedoms, can continue to contribute to progressive American democracy if it renders due accord to political authority. A free and viable society requires, as its basis, a level of order that provides the individual with peace and security in his constructive endeavors and in his possessions. The conservatives have, of course, always recognized this. Commenting on the importance of order, justice, and freedom to the American people, Russell Kirk has argued that, of these, "order has primacy: for justice cannot be enforced until a tolerable civil social order is attained, nor can freedom be anything better than violence until order gives us laws."[8] And Philip Abbott has pointed directly to the liberal failings in this respect with his charge that "the liberal is without a conceptual vocabulary to justify the state. . . ."[9] But in view of the current political malaise, liberals must come to recognize that government can act firmly and directively and yet remain democratically responsible; and, in fact, a number of important, liberally respectable, twentieth-century thinkers have held this view.

Relating directly to the importance of a government capable of acting firmly is the mounting evidence that the social divisions and external crises faced by the American nation are becoming too serious for the "government as usual" approach to be allowed to continue. Anyone familiar with the political catastrophes of the twentieth century is well aware that weak government is an invitation to totalitarianism. Americans must insist that liberals reorder their theoretical priorities if they are to remain politically respectable, for a government without sufficient ideological props to enable it to act is, in the present era, an invitation to social upheaval and chaos. In a very real, although not widely acknowledged, sense, human freedom is at stake. Continued refusal to construct a framework for a viable political order that is at the same time democratic will render Americans prey by default to systems of political order that have wreaked immeasurable human suffering.

Here, the liberal tradition and its relationship to the question of governmental authority will be examined through chronological analysis of what might be termed "political ideas." These ideas have originated in the systematic considerations of politics produced by the seminal thinkers in the Anglo-American tradition. More important for the purposes of this analysis, however, is the fact that these ideas have continued to live outside of a thinker's works and his close circle of followers. In short, they have become part of the nation's political ideology. The approach to a thinker's ideas will be concerned with what he wrote and with what those words meant within the social and cultural context in which they were written. Injecting today's meanings into the words of the past has no constructive purpose in the study of political thought outside of the subjective pleasures derived from self-constructed fantasies. On the

---

[8] Russell Kirk, *The Roots of American Order* (LaSalle, IL.: Open Court, 1974), p. 6.
[9] Philip Abbott, *The Shotgun Behind the Door* (Athens, GA.: University of Georgia Press, 1976), p. 10.

other hand, the beliefs of a culture and the social relationships that exist are often inarticulate assumptions of a thinker and keys to the interpretation of his ideas. Thus, liberal thinkers have at times tacitly accepted the validity of powerful government authority or restrictive social arrangements while writing in what appear today to be highly individualistic terms.

Liberalism as a system of ideas has, of course, been much broader than political theory. Its greatest thinkers have been important philosophers who were as interested in ascertaining the means to "truth" as in providing a rationale for political action. The epistemological element in liberalism has consistently been attracted to the methods and achievements of the physical sciences, and the important liberal thinkers in the philosophical sense have inevitably described their positions as scientific. In this respect, liberalism has successfully obtained public approbation through its ability to associate itself with advances in the physical sciences. At the same time, infatuation with scientific progress has given liberals tremendous confidence in the capacity of human reason, and if there is one element that has characterized liberalism throughout the past three and one-half centuries, it has been a faith in the ability of men to change society for the better. Reinforcing the longevity of liberalism in the Anglo-American world has been its ability to dovetail with economic change. Thus, liberalism has often been seen as the ideology of reform and revolution. Liberal thinkers such as Hobbes, Bentham, and Dewey have emphatically rejected the importance of tradition and relied on the power of the human mind in the here and now to construct a more perfect social world.

The philosophical positions taken by liberal thinkers have had important political ramifications. The eclipse of the static Newtonian physics by the evolutionary doctrines of Darwin, especially in American intellectual circles, issued ultimately in a revised estimate of the worth of the pursuit of definitive truth. In this country, truth came to be seen as relative to an individual's perspective, and the importance of science for social policy became its methodology, not its conclusions. With this change in philosophical foundations, liberalism moved from an attachment to relatively static political assumptions to a position justifying continual change, a stance highly congenial to the reform orientation of major American liberal thinkers. Once truth was seen as relative, it was but a short step to asserting that social arrangements and, of course, their values were relative as well. It was with this move that liberal ideological rhetoric initiated the process of social divisiveness that has left government without stable social foundations or legitimacy and society without direction.

The formative influences that have determined the configuration of those liberal ideas that have conditioned the American experience since the Civil War have been primarily English in origin. Although the conditions of seventeenth-century England are far removed from the cognitive horizons of Americans experiencing the 1980s, important ideas first propounded by the major liberal thinkers of that bygone era are still to be found among those fundamental values that remain in America. These include confidence in human rationality, an individualistic conception of society, rejection of the authority of tradition, acceptance of science as an ultimate standard of value, and the concept of constitutional government. Even the egalitarianism that has become such an important part of American liberalism can be traced to the essential equality assigned to individuals by Hobbes. In America, French Enlightenment thought inceptionally had some influence politically, particularly in the construction of formal governmental institutions; however, the philosophical assumptions of the ante-bellum period later paled in comparison to the influence exercised by ideas stemming from Darwin and evolutionary theory generally. Furthermore, the political processes justified by the reform liberalism derived from these newer views have undermined and circumvented the institutional interactions originally anticipated by the formal constitutional structures.

But it would not be accurate, even at this early point in the discussion, to speak entirely in terms of philosophical currents or their political emanations, for liberalism as an ideological force has often been supported by forms of social control that have gone without philosophical or public articulation. Concepts of pervasive social control surfaced briefly in the thought of Bentham but were quickly submerged by the ensuing waves of laissez faire ideas. As with Hegel's owl of Minerva that took flight only with the gathering of dusk, commentators on social development are just now beginning to understand the unarticulated forces of social control that were operative during what has been seen as a period of unrestrained capitalism. Their findings suggest rather strongly what liberals of the past century have been unwilling to admit, namely that liberal ideas have been the beneficiaries of rather powerful forms of social control.

The approach taken here is intended to be one of interpretation not of reinterpretation. The justification for this effort is that it focuses in systematic fashion on an aspect of liberal thought that has not received much examination. Because of this difference in orientation, new insights and an alternative, perhaps more useful, understanding of liberalism's role in western culture should emerge. In constructing this alternative view, I do not, however, intend to stray very far from the words and contexts of the thinkers and ideas examined.

This study assumes that the dominant ideological forces in America since at least the Civil War have been fundamentally liberal. In their basic assumptions, both the proponents of laissez faire and the advocates of increased state interventionism have been liberals. Both have stressed the value of individual rationality and freedom; their differences have been over the means for achieving the greatest individual development. Focus on this difference in approaches, rather than on the similar basic ideological positions, has sometimes led to the confusion of labelling the laissez faire individualists "conservative" and the state interventionists "liberal." Following this method of classification to its logical conclusion leads to the absurd position that Alexander Hamilton, a proponent of activist government, was a liberal and Thomas Jefferson, an advocate of limited government, a conservative. With the exception of the pre-Civil War South and the Puritans, conservative assumptions, which emphasize tradition, limited human capacity, and the need for controlling human passions, simply have not played an important political role in the development of the American nation.

This investigation begins with consideration of the giants of Anglo-American liberalism—Hobbes and Locke. Both Hobbes and Locke were responding to the tremendous cultural upheavals of the seventeenth century, and their views were to be influential on the ensuing development of liberalism. Liberalism's concern with economic matters and the relevance of science for political and social relationships can be traced to the importance that Hobbes and Locke attached to these subjects. Both men reflected in their thought the significance that seventeenth-century Englishmen gave to advances in the physical sciences led by Newton and to the increasing importance of trade as epitomized by aggressive entrepreneurs. Traditional explanations of man's place in society that were adequate for a feudal order based on religious beliefs and a static social order no longer sufficed in an era that had witnessed the Protestant Reformation, Newton's explanation of the universe, and the execution of Charles I. Hobbes and Locke remained important to liberalism because they suggested viable theoretical structures encompassing the changes faced by Englishmen of their time and succeeding generations.

Hobbes provides the first and most thorough statement of the English liberal position. In fact, an important recent treatment of the western philosophical tradition argues that he is one of the two originators of "modern philosophy."[10] Locke lacked the logical rigor of Hobbes, but his political and epistemological works were to have continuing influence among liberals. From Hobbes and Locke, the narrative then traces English attitudes toward political authority through the eighteenth century. The thought of the utilitarians Bentham and James Mill and of Burke receives comparative treatment in terms of alternative approaches to the theoretical basis for authority. For Americans, however, these views

---

[10] Richard Rorty, *Philosophy and the Mirror of Nature* (Princeton: Princeton University Press, 1980), p. 131. The other thinker so credited by Rorty is Descartes.

were to be overshadowed by the position taken by Herbert Spencer somewhat later in the nineteenth century.

With Spencer's thought, consideration of the liberal tradition shifts naturally to the American context. It is incontrovertible that contemporary American liberal thought stems primarily from the tremendous changes wrought after the Civil War. In every area of American life, the differences between the ante-bellum and post-bellum eras were qualitatively and quantitatively significant. Technologically, the country became an industrial society. Scientifically, the ideas of Darwin and advances in physics had a tremendous impact. Culturally and socially, Darwin and Spencer provided impetus for dramatically changed ways of looking at the world and the individual's place in it. Even the fundamental law of the land, the U.S. Constitution, changed with the addition of the Fourteenth Amendment and the resulting protections for corporate capitalism and, much later, for individual liberties that were found to be encompassed therein.

The ensuing conflict between the forces of individualism and state interventionism did not produce a conceptual framework for the exercise of governmental authority because both positions were narrowly rooted in liberalism and thus suffered from that ideology's blindness to its indebtedness to forces of social control. The competing positions were clearly presented in the works of the major thinkers, but they were also reflected in public policy, particularly that formulated by the U.S. Supreme Court. The Supreme Court decisions are valuable for this study because they are the law of the land and provide specific statements as to the basis for that law. Additionally, the Court, often considered the most politically insulated branch of government, has reflected the debilitating effects of liberalism on government authority.

While there have been important thinkers in the twentieth century who have been able to distance themselves from the two major ideological positions and have criticized their failure to provide a basis for governmental authority, these individuals in turn have not been successful in constructing persuasive formulations to fill the theoretical lacunae that they have discovered. Ironically, the relative success of the state interventionists in disposing of laissez faire in the economic sphere has been accompanied by an increase in laissez fairism in social areas that has seriously undermined government authority and at the same time made the need for such authority more pressing. Today, government remains the one social institution with the potential for conserving the gains of liberalism and for maintaining the social stability necessary for their enjoyment. Given the proper ideological resources, it can still act within a democratic framework to provide social direction and yet restrain itself from undue interference in the lives of its citizens.

The Origins of Liberalism

ENGLISH SOCIETY AND POLITICAL IDEAS

Although they are far removed in time and condition from seventeenth-century England, Americans remain heavily indebted to many of the political ideas of that era. Responding to the dramatic social and cultural changes of their time, seventeenth-century English thinkers constructed theoretical positions that were to serve as the basis for the development of liberal thought over the next three centuries.

Thomas Hobbes: The Authoritarian Foundations of Liberalism

One thinker dominates the beginnings of Anglo-American liberal thought, and that individual is Thomas Hobbes. Hobbes's theoretical system ranges from discussion of the forces governing the universe and epistemological explanations to the implementation of legal directives. In the scope of his thought, Hobbes was of a piece with the great systems builders of the seventeenth century.[1] He ranks as the greatest of Anglo-American political philosophers, liberal or otherwise. The expanse of his thought, the clarity of his ideas and expression, and the rigor of his logic remain impressive even after three centuries.

Drawing on contemporary ideas about science and geometry, Hobbes literally reconstructed the assumptions and methodology of political thought. In this effort, he rejected the constraints posed by tradition, custom, and religion and freed the individual *qua* individual to make subjective judgments as to the validity of institutions. It was his atomistic statement of the individual and the judgmental status regarding the humanly constructed edifices of society that he granted the individual that were to stimulate much of the recognizable thrust of later liberalism.

---

[1] George H. Sabine, *A History of Political Theory* (Third edition; New York: Holt, Rinehart and Winston, 1961), p. 426.

Of course, there was another, authoritarian, side to Hobbes, and certainly he can not be accused of subterfuge in his presentation of this aspect of his thought. His description of the position of the absolute sovereign was characteristically forthright.

> ...This is the Generation of that great LEVIATHAN, or rather (to speak more reverently) of that *Mortall God*, to which wee own under the *Immortal God*, our peace and defence. For by this Authoritie... he hath the use of so much Power and Strength conferred on him, that by terror thereof, he is inabled to forme the wills of them all ...[2]

> ...As in the presence of the Master, the Servants are equall, and without any honour at all; So are the Subjects, in the presence of the Soveraign....[3]

It is true that Hobbes believed that sovereign power over the political commonwealth, if not attained by conquest, rested inceptionally on the voluntary consent of the governed, but he was emphatic in asserting that, once granted, this power was absolute.[4]

Hobbes states at the conclusion of *Leviathan* that his effort was "occasioned by the disorders of the present time..."[5] and in retrospect it would appear that these disorders were sufficient to explain many of his positions. Not only was England rent by the vicious civil war, but the continent to which Hobbes fled during the decade of the forties was suffering, during this period, from the depredations of the Thirty Years War. Hobbes's consistent concern was that of achieving peace. "*That every man, ought to endeavor Peace, as farre as he has hope of obtaining it*..." was, in Hobbes's opinion, the "fundamentall Law of Nature."[6] Behind his theory of the state was his clearly stated goal of avoiding a state, or condition, of "warre."[7]

The foundation of Hobbes's *Leviathan* lies in his opinion of human nature, and here C. B. Macpherson's close reading of Hobbes is helpful. Macpherson suggests that Hobbes considered his description of man in the state of nature to be that of the human condition wherever it is without the restraint of law.[8] He points out that, at the beginning of *De Cive*, Hobbes discusses the individual in society and in his natural condition and appears to see the same basic drives operant in each state. In

---

[2] Thomas Hobbes, *Leviathan*. Edited with introduction by C. B. Macpherson (Baltimore: Penguin Books, 1968 [First published 1651]), p. 227.

[3] *Ibid.*, p. 238.

[4] *Ibid.*, pp. 228–239.

[5] *Ibid.*, p. 728.

[6] *Ibid.*, p. 190.

[7] *Ibid.*, pp. 185–188; Thomas Hobbes, "The Citizen" in Thomas Hobbes, *Man and Citizen*. Thomas Hobbes's *De Homine* [1658] translated by Charles T. Wood, T. S. K. Scott-Craig, and Bernard Gert and *De Cive* [1651]. Edited with introduction by Bernard Gert (Garden City, N.Y.: Anchor Books, 1972), pp. 117–119.

[8] C. B. Macpherson, *The Political Theory of Possessive Individualism* (New York: Oxford University Press, 1962), pp. 22, 25.

society, men act from desire for gain and glory.[9] Their attachment to civil society is engendered by their fear of each other, a fear that Hobbes demonstrates with examples from civil society in a discussion very similar to that which occurs later in *Leviathan*.[10] The key to peace in both of these works is a common powerful authority, and Hobbes appears to say in *Leviathan* that, without such an authority, society must degenerate into a state of civil war, a condition with which Hobbes was all too familiar.

> ...Howsoever, it may be perceived what manner of life there would be, where there were no common Power to feare; by the manner of life which men that have formerly lived under a peacefull government, use to degenerate into, in a civill Warre.[11]

Based on these reflections, it seems reasonable to conclude that Hobbes saw man's nature as a constant threat to the peace and security of society.

Because, in his famous words, the life of men without authority to govern them would be "solitary, poore, nasty, brutish, and short,"[12] Hobbes believed that men are at least sufficiently rational to remove themselves from this condition by granting absolute power to a sovereign authority. With this assumption, Hobbes broke with previous philosophical tradition and instituted what Thomas A. Spragens has termed a "paradigm transformation" in political thought.[13] The social foundations constructed from the axioms of religion, tradition, and custom were seriously weakened by Hobbes's clear articulation of the position that government legitimacy in its origins stemmed from the perceived needs of those who founded it. With this conceptual move, the possibility of a standard for political judgment based on the desires of the subjective individual was raised, an occurrence that in retrospect can be seen as a logical outcome of the individualized judgment encouraged in the religious sphere by the Protestant Reformation.

Perhaps of parallel importance in Hobbes's thought are the equalitarian elements in his assumptions, elements that contrast rather markedly with the views of John Locke. In his description of the state of nature, Hobbes projected a relative equality of individuals in terms of strength and what he terms "prudence." The latter attribute is more equally distributed among men than strength, for it is "but Experience; which equall time, equally bestowes on all men, in those things they equally apply themselves unto...."[14] Hobbes notes that men may indeed see them-

---

[9] Hobbes, "Citizen," pp. 111–112.
[10] *Ibid.*, pp. 113–114; cf. Hobbes, *Leviathan,* pp. 183–188.
[11] Hobbes, *Leviathan*, p. 187.
[12] *Ibid.*, p. 186.
[13] Thomas A. Spragens, *The Politics of Motion* (Lexington, Kentucky: University of Kentucky Press, 1973), pp. 203–205.
[14] Hobbes, *Leviathan*, p. 183.

selves unequal in this faculty, but this opinion is "but a vain conceipt of ones owne wisdome, which almost all men think they have in a greater degree, than the Vulgar; that is, than all men but themselves, and a few others, whome by Fame, or for concurring with themselves, they approve...."[15] Obviously, Hobbes's estimate of mankind is not high, but he argues that individuals do have a certain minimal ability to judge their own best interests. "A plain husband-man is more Prudent in affaires of his own house, than a Privy Counseller in the affaires of another man."[16] Thus, when men decide to enter into a civil society, the agreement to do so is one of "every man with every man."[17] The choice of who the sovereign shall be may be made by a majority, but all have voluntarily participated in giving up their rights, other than that of self-preservation, to that person or persons.[18]

Unfortunately, the low-key treatment given to Hobbes's position on authority reflects contemporary liberalism's unwillingness to come to grips with the issue of authority. Where this aspect of his thought is not simply ignored or quickly brushed aside, the treatment of it often follows the tack suggested by that early liberal, James Harrington, who suggested that the leviathan separated from economic power could be "but a name or mere spitfrog."[19] Sheldon Wolin is particularly vehement that Hobbes's view of authority was superficial and that a sovereign of the Hobbesian variety could not be expected to govern effectively.[20] Others have echoed this view.[21]

It was through his combination of science, language, and power that Hobbes was able to conceive of an absolute sovereign who would be far more powerful than critics of Hobbes's idea have been willing to allow. John Danford has shown that Hobbes saw himself as constructing the framework for a scientific politics, or in his words, "morall or civill philosophy." Previous discourses on politics had been subversive of political order because, without commonly accepted definitions, they engendered controversies that reflected little more than the subjective opinions of those involved.[22] In particular, religion had prevented the scientific development of language in the social and political areas by proliferating

---

[15] *Ibid.*, pp. 183–184.

[16] *Ibid.*, p. 138.

[17] *Ibid.*, pp. 227, 228–229.

[18] *Ibid.*, pp. 228–232.

[19] Quoted in Sabine, *op. cit.*, p. 499. Most of the opposition from Hobbes's contemporaries focused on the rationalist basis for authority that he urged, not on the need for authority itself.

[20] Sheldon Wolin, *Politics and Vision* (Boston: Little, Brown, 1960), pp. 275–276.

[21] See Lee C. McDonald, *Western Political Theory* (New York: Harcourt, Brace & World, 1968), pp. 319–320.

[22] John W. Danford, *Wittgenstein and Political Philosophy* (Chicago: University of Chicago Press, 1978), pp. 18–19, 48.

words without commonly accepted referents.[23] Hobbes believed that, in the methods of geometry, he had discovered the clue to formulating a science of politics. The terms of geometry were accepted as having the same meanings by all who used them. Utilizing these terms, one could proceed on the basis of accepted rules toward the resolution of a problem and reach a conclusion that would be recognized as valid by anyone knowledgeable in geometry. Thus, Hobbes argued that a science of politics must also have, as its foundation, words with universally accepted meanings.[24]

Through control of language, Hobbesian man would be in a position to construct a new political reality for himself and his fellow citizens. Hobbes saw a science of politics as having the potential for being more precise and certain than the physical sciences because man lives and knows the relationships that he uses language to describe.[25] In essence, he was arguing that, with the achievement of a settled language of political discourse, a political system of peace and stability based on scientific principles should be possible. It seems likely that Hobbes believed that he was offering such a system with the model detailed in *Leviathan*. Wolin seems to take a similar position even though he fails to see how Hobbes's science could have been related to increasing the sovereign's power.

> ...The importance of language and rules was written into the very substance of the Hobbesian political philosophy, coloring his conception of the state of nature, the form taken by the covenant, the position of sovereign and subject, the status of law and morals, and the role of reason in politics.[26]

Clearly, government in a political society where terms such as "justice" and "injustice" have uniformly accepted meanings would lack much of the controversy that we have come to expect from the political process. Essentially, Hobbes contended that through the propagation of true doctrine the sovereign must create meaning and values for his subjects.

The primary goal of Hobbes's sovereign is peace, and it seems likely that a scientifically useful language that eliminated controversies of a seditious nature was envisaged by Hobbes as an important tool for governance. Hobbes states that effective governance requires a knowledge of principles comparable to those of mathematics and not know-

---

[23] *Ibid.*, p. 38.

[24] *Ibid.*, pp. 19, 28, 33, 41; John W. Danford, "The Problem of Language in Hobbes's Political Science," *The Journal of Politics*, XLII (February, 1980), 127–129. Wolin also remarks on Hobbes's reliance on geometry, but he and Danford disagree on whether geometry is properly empirical and legitimately part of the scientific method. See Wolin, *op. cit.*, p. 251 and cf. Danford, "The Problem," pp. 117–118.

[25] Danford, "The Problem," p. 131.

[26] Wolin, *op. cit.*, p. 253.

able without study and thought, efforts necessary for acquiring scientific skill.[27]

> ... The skill of making, and maintaining Common-wealths, consisteth in certain Rules, as doth Arithmetique and Geometry; not (as Tennis-play) on Practice only: which Rules, neither poor men have the leisure, nor men that have had the leisure, have hitherto had the curiosity, or the method to find out.[28]

He asserts at another point that "*Reason* is the *pace*; Encrease of *Science*, the *way*; and the Benefit of man-kind the *end*...."[29] When Hobbes addresses himself to the objection that no commonwealth based on absolute authority had been known to exist previously, he turns again to the lack of a science of politics. The states of the past, he asserts, could not have been based on scientific bases because language was not used in a scientifically constructive fashion, but in *Leviathan* such principles have now been set forth.[30] In the conclusion to Part II of *Leviathan*, he again makes this point.

> ... Science of Natural Justice, is the onely Science necessary for Soveraigns ... neither *Plato*, nor any other Philosopher hitherto, hath put into order, and sufficiently, or probably proved all the Theoremes of Morall doctrine, that men may learn thereby, both how to govern, and how to obey ...[31]

Throughout *Leviathan*, Hobbes's discussion is in terms of the absolute sovereign applying the principles of reason, or science, through the civil laws. The "dictates of Reason" are "Conclusions, or Theoremes concerning what conduceth to the conservation and defence of themselves [men]"[32] and "the Science of them, is the true and onely Moral Philosophy...."[33]

There is then more to Hobbes's sovereign than mere fear or terror, although Hobbes does often refer to the importance of the sword and fear for making men obey. Generally, however, Hobbes is arguing that through the principles of valid moral philosophy, which include language manipulation, the sovereign should be able to educate his subjects as to the wisdom of his possession of absolute power. He specifically recognizes that workable absolute authority must ultimately rest on the citizens' acceptance of its rationale. It is the sovereign's duty to see that his subjects "be diligently and truly taught; because they cannot be maintained by an Civill Law, or terrour of legal punishment...."[34] Toward this end, the sovereign has the right to control the doctrines and opinions of his subjects, for "the Actions of men proceed from their Opinions;

---

[27] Hobbes, *Leviathan*, p. 183.
[28] *Ibid.*, p. 261.
[29] *Ibid.*, p. 116.
[30] *Ibid.*, pp. 377–378.
[31] *Ibid.*, pp. 407–408.
[32] *Ibid.*, pp. 216, 217.
[33] *Ibid.*, pp. 215–216.
[34] *Ibid.*, p. 377.

and in the well governing of Opinions, consisteth the well governing of mens Actions, in order to their Peace, and Concord. . . ."[35] The absolute power of the sovereign is dependent on his retaining control of the militia, the supply of money, and "the government of doctrines."[36] At other places in *Leviathan*, Hobbes rails against false teachers and advocates state utilization of "publique instruction" to control the beliefs of its citizens.[37]

Hobbes argued that through the control of definitions and their use in language, political values could be universally determined. Terms such as "justice" and "liberty" would then have settled meanings for everyone within the state. Hobbes expected the sovereign to be conversant with this approach to eliminating political controversy, and he was careful to endow the sovereign with the means for implementing the language and values most conducive to peace and stability in the commonwealth.

In *Leviathan*, Hobbes was consistent and firm in the pursuit of one goal, the institution of a political system that could provide internal peace and stability. He seems to have been willing to utilize any form of political and social control that would aid in this effort. Thus, although his arguments regarding the political importance of language carry heavy totalitarian undertones, they are a reasonable consequence of his aversion to controversy and subversion within the state. There is then every reason to believe that when Hobbes used the term "absolute power," he meant exactly that. For him, the well-ordered commonwealth required the political integration of science, language, and power by the Sovereign. Succeeding liberal thought tended to submerge concern for strong authority under a consideration for individual rights, and the full ramifications of Hobbes's sovereign were lost in this transposition of interests. If later thinkers had dealt more fully and directly with this aspect of Hobbes's thought, coherent, and workable alternatives to his position on this point might have evolved.

Despite conceptual problems, Hobbes's *Leviathan* remains the most thorough statement for secularly based authority in the English-speaking world. His recognition of the power of language usage was a remarkable insight into an aspect of politics that has undergone extensive exploitation by American ideological groupings, especially, in the latter twentieth century. Just as he rejected the ruminations of past political thinkers as engendering political strife and controversy, so he rejected the previous sources of legitimacy for political authority as incapable of providing internal peace and stability. In Hobbes's system, the needs of con-

---

[35] *Ibid.*, p. 233.

[36] *Ibid.*, p. 236.

[37] *Ibid.*, pp. 291, 340, 376–379. Compare Warrender's statement that "[t]he function of the civil sovereign is not to create moral principles nor even to educate the citizen. . . ." Howard Warrender, *The Political Philosophy of Hobbes* (Oxford: Clarendon Press, 1957), p. 143.

crete individuals became the standards by which political authority should be judged. At the same time that he cast aside traditional sources of legitimacy in favor of individual needs, he imposed a system of political absolutism on these individuals. Hobbes did not turn from the authorities of the past in order to free the individual. He turned from them because they were ineffective in providing political stability. He turned to the individual because he was wise enough to see that a political system hoping for some degree of long-term stability must find support in its citizens. For it is citizens who rebel, who instigate civil war, not the voices of the past nor even He who as Immortal God stands above that Mortal God, the Leviathan. Unfortunately for the coherent development of a theory of political authority in liberal thought, Hobbes's immediate successors tended to take the need for strong authority as a given and concentrated instead on articulating individualistic values.

John Locke: Political Authority and Property

John Locke has not provided us in one work with a single statement of his political philosophy that has the comprehensive range of Hobbes's *Leviathan*. Locke was more intimately involved in the English politics of his day and his major political work, *Two Treatises on Government* (1690), appears to have been occasioned by the ideological needs of his political allies. Locke's partisan political activities, and the rather truncated nature of his *Two Treatises*, force the contemporary interpreter of his thought to give careful attention to the socio-political context in which he wrote and from which he derived his assumptions. His failure to produce a work that developed his thought from fundamental epistemological positions through a discussion of political institutions and the position of the citizen has contributed to the accusations that he was a confused and contradictory thinker. On the other hand, the ambiguity of his works may have been an important factor in their popularity and longevity. Thus, subsequent interpretations of his ideas have portrayed him as a spokesman for inviolable rights against the state when analysis of his political writings in relation to the cultural and social context within which they were produced indicates that he was in fact an advocate of strong governmental power.

Although there were important differences between Hobbes and himself, Locke could not and did not envision government as broadly based or responsive to the whims of the populace. In this respect, his thought continues the Hobbesian concern for strong governmental authority within the state. The misinterpretations of Locke on this point have issued from his failure to explicate thoroughly the bases for his political ideas and from his tendency to express himself in absolute or universalistic terms. When transferred to contexts different from that of seventeenth-century England, these statements rather easily succumbed to the depredations of those bent on constructing egalitarian political societies. Locke's reluctance to provide a clear, comprehensive rationale for the strong governmental authority that he and his contemporary English readers assumed began a degenerative process in the theoretical foundations for authority that was to culminate in liberalism's current quandary as to its conceptual basis.

In 1660, Locke clearly preferred a ruler with absolute and arbitrary power. In an unpublished manuscript from that year, he wrote that "the *Supreme Magistrate* of every Nation what way soever created must necessarily have an *absolute & arbitrary* power over all the indifferent actions of his people...."[38] Macpherson places some importance on the term "indifferent actions" as those outside the dictates of natural law.[39] But a later quotation from the same manuscript indicates that Locke intended, just as did Hobbes, that in civil society the magistrate would have absolute power.

> ...It is yet the unalterable condicon of Society & Govermt that every particular man must unavoidable part with his right to his liberty & intrust the magistrate with as full a power over all his actions as he himself hath, it being otherwise impossible that any one should be subject to the commands of an other who retains the free disposure of himself, & is master of an equall liberty....[40]

W. von Leyden notes that, just before the Restoration, Locke expressed "deep contempt for mankind" and argues convincingly that the supreme power that Locke advocated at this time covered all of men's actions. When the sovereign implemented God's will, men were bound by conscience to obey; when he acted in "matters indifferent," they were still bound to obey although they retained freedom of conscience.[41]

In the *Second Treatise*, Locke's treatment of political authority differs from that in his 1660 unpublished manuscript. The modifications in his position may have been heavily influenced by his political affiliations in 1679-1681, the period during which most of the *Two Treatises* was written. John Dunn, for example, states that Locke's close association with the Earl of Shaftesbury's efforts to have Charles II's brother, a Catholic, ex-

---

[38] Quoted in Macpherson, *op. cit.*, p. 258; see also W. von Leyden, "Introduction" in W. von Leyden (ed.), *John Locke: Essays on the Law of Nature* (Oxford: Clarendon Press, 1965), pp. 26–27. On the use of the word "arbitrary," see Peter Laslett, "Introduction" in John Locke, *Two Treatises of Government*. Edited with introduction by Peter Laslett (Revised edition; New York: New American Library, 1965 [First published by Cambridge University Press, 1963]), p. 32.

[39] Macpherson, *op. cit.*, pp. 259–260.

[40] Quoted in *ibid.*, p. 259. Macpherson concludes that at this time Locke was writing in support of the return of the Stuarts. *Ibid.*, p. 261.

[41] Von Leyden, *op. cit.*, pp. 17, 26, 28–29. Von Leyden does not address the issue of a ruler who acts contrary to God's will, although he later notes Locke's allowance that men are not bound to obey a tyrant. *Ibid.*, p. 51. Laslett suggests that the uneasy conditions in the period from Cromwell's death to the Restoration caused Locke to turn to strong governmental authority. Laslett, *op. cit.*, p. 32.

cluded from the line of accession to the throne caused him to frame his arguments so that they would have particular appeal to the landed gentry. Despite the widespread fear of popery at this time, the Anglican Church's opposition to revolt remained highly influential. Moreover, the upheavals of the decade of the forties caused many to fear the tangible social consequences of another sustained effort at opposing the crown. If Shaftesbury was to be successful, the landed gentry had to be persuaded that action against the crown was not a mortal sin and a sure route to anarchy and social suicide.[42] Viewed in this light, the arguments of the *Two Treatises* focus directly on the issues of concern to the landed gentry.[43]

In the *First Treatise*, Locke spares no effort in seeking to demolish Filmer's arguments in support of the divine right of kingship. In the *Second Treatise*, he focuses on the legislative power and its responsibility in a manner permeated with the values of social stability and the primacy of private property.

The popularized account of Locke's ideas notes the importance of property, but it does not begin to reflect adequately the pervasive influence of property in the social fabric of Locke's England or the role that the propertied played in his assumptions about political activity in general. The definitive character of property as an indicator of social and political power was a given of Locke's time, and his exposition of the political in the *Second Treatise* revolves around this fact.

England of the latter seventeenth century was a rigidly stratified society with the nobility and men of great wealth at the top. Below these, the social orders dropped rapidly in influence and prestige with the majority of the population—day laborers, servants, and the poor—at or close to ground zero. In the words of Caroline Robbins,

> ... a ruling class and an uneducated and unrepresented majority were for a long time taken for granted ... by 'people' most seventeenth-century Republicans had meant people of some state and consequence in the community. Cobblers, tinkers, or fishermen were not people but *scum* to Whigs like James Tyrrell—who used the term—to Locke, Withers, and Trenchard. . . .[44]

Macpherson quotes R. H. Tawney on the harsher treatment that the industrial proletariat tended to receive from writers of this period.[45]

---

[42] John Dunn, *Political Obligation in Its Historical Context* (Cambridge: Cambridge University Press, 1980), pp. 54–57.

[43] Leo Strauss also notes the contemporary grounding of the *Two Treatises*. In his words, "[i]n the *Treatise*, it is less Locke the philosopher than Locke the Englishman who addresses not philosophers, but Englishmen. . . ." Leo Strauss, *Natural Right and History* (Chicago: University of Chicago Press, 1953), pp. 220–221.

[44] Caroline Robbins, *The Eighteenth-Century Commonwealthman* (Cambridge, MA.: Harvard University Press, 1961), p. 16.

[45] Macpherson, *op. cit.*, p. 228.

Peter Laslett states that "in the world we have lost...an entity like 'England' lives its whole life within the confines of a small, select minority...." He goes on to say that even a Leveller leader such as John Lilburne in 1646 could "say things which seemed to affect every living individual without his actually contemplating more than a small portion of them...."[46] The level of elite consensus on fundamental political, social, and religious values was sufficiently high to allow for the expiration of the Licensing Act for the press in 1695. On this point, Christopher Hill remarks that "the opinion-formers of this society censored themselves. Nothing got into print which frightened the men of property...."[47]

Dunn notes that Locke had no intention of threatening the power configuration of the hierarchical social system in which he wrote.[48] But Macpherson appears to have carried this line of interpretation the farthest. He argues that Locke was so imbued with the social values of his day that he simply could not conceive of the propertyless having a political role. He sees Locke's state of nature as evolving through two stages:[49] the first, a state of relative equality without money; the second, one of haves and have-nots created by the introduction of money.[50] Money allows for the accumulation of wealth far beyond what one needs for personal use,[51] and its introduction into the state of nature inevitably engenders economic inequality. It is the men of property, or the industrious and the rational, who have substantial interests to protect, who actively covenant to enter into civil society, and it is they who subsequently govern.[52] The laboring classes could never be full political members of society, primarily because their hand-to-mouth existence prevented them from fully developing their rational faculties. The unemployed were seen in an even harsher light by Locke, who seems to have believed that their idleness stemmed from moral depravity.[53]

Macpherson supports much of his argument from sources other than the *Second Treatise*, the notable exception being his well-known "serf and turf" citation. In his discussion of the appropriation of private property, Locke argued that one's labor expended in appropriating an

---

[46] Peter Laslett, *The World We Have Lost* (Second edition; [n.p.]: Charles Scribner's Sons, 1973), p. 189.

[47] Christopher Hill, *The World Turned Upside Down* (New York: Viking Press, 1973), p. 311.

[48] Dunn, *op. cit.*, pp. 60–61.

[49] Cf., John Locke, *An Essay Concerning the True Original, Extent and End of Civil Government* [1690] in Ernest Barker (ed.), *Social Contract* (New York: Oxford University Press, 1962), ¶4–15, 16–24. [Hereinafter cited as *Civil Government*.]

[50] Strauss also seems to indicate that two states in the state of nature are derivable from Locke. The first being one of "penury." Strauss, *op. cit.*, p. 238.

[51] Locke, *Civil Government*, ¶36, 45, 47, 50.

[52] *Ibid.*, ¶34; Macpherson, *op. cit.*, pp. 209–210.

[53] See Macpherson, *op. cit.*, pp. 221–229.

object entitled one to that object. By way of example, he offered the following hypothetical situations.

> ... Thus, the grass my horse has bit, the turfs my servant has cut, and the ore I have digged in any place, where I have a right to them in common with others, become my property without the assignation or consent of any body. . . .[54]

Unfortunately, it is not clear from the context of this quotation if Locke is speaking of the state of nature. If he was, Macpherson's interpretation of Locke generally would be strongly reinforced. As the quote stands, it is clear that Locke had absolutely no inclination to suggest that because the servant had dug the turfs, they were by right his. The servant is seen as but an extension of the person of property, receiving less direct benefit from the turfs than does the horse from the grass that it has "bit."

Macpherson's central contention is that Locke had a very low opinion of the propertyless and could not have imagined these sorts of people engaging in the normal political activities of seventeenth-century England.[55] Peter Laslett adds support to this view.

> ... In his published works he [Locke] showed himself the determined enemy of beggars and the idle poor, who existed, he thought, because of "the relaxation of discipline and the corruption of manners." He even implied that a working family had no right to expect its children to be at leisure after the age of three.[56]

Obviously, Locke was a strong proponent of the work ethic for those without property or other wealth.

Thus, the evidence is reasonably convincing that Locke assumed the dominance of the propertied in his England. These individuals would, of course, be in basic agreement on the fundamental values of the day, as evidenced by their belief that censorship of the press through government was no longer needed. These assumptions by Locke allowed him to argue in support of strong government without fear that the values that he held dear would be seriously threatened. Locke's political thought, then, must be seen not as a statement for the egalitarian representation and protection of all individuals in society but as a justification for the exercise of extensive governmental authority by the propertied few. He was intent on freeing these few from the abuses of the monarchy and had no interest in providing a rationale for the masses' rise to political ascendency.

In several places in the *Second Treatise*, Locke declares in unambiguous language that the legislative power is the supreme power in govern-

---

[54] Locke, *Civil Government*, ¶28.
[55] It should be noted that Macpherson concludes that Locke believed that all Englishmen were equal in their basic right to life and liberty. Macpherson, *op. cit.*, pp. 243, 247–250.
[56] Laslett, "Introduction," p. 56.

ment. "This legislative is not only the supreme power of the commonwealth, but sacred and unalterable in the hands where the community have once placed it...."[57] Although the legislative be supreme, says Locke, yet there are limits on its powers. At first glance, such a position appears to be obviously illogical, but Locke was arguing that the legislative power was supreme among the institutions of government. As he states at a later point, "the legislative being only a fiduciary power to act for certain ends, there remains still in the people a supreme power to remove or alter the legislative...."[58]

Those specific limitations that Locke would impose on the legislative power appear, on close examination, to be essentially procedural in nature. I can find in the *Second Treatise* no substantive limits that Locke places on the legislative power other than the general requirement that it must act for the public good,[59] a requirement no different from that imposed by Hobbes on his sovereign. By acting in the interest of the public, the legislative power must not be exercised arbitrarily or contrary to God's will.[60] Laws must be duly promulgated. "And, therefore, whatever form the commonwealth is under, the ruling power ought to govern by declared and received laws, and not by extemporary dictates and undetermined resolutions...."[61] Locke's concern here is not absolute power but absolute arbitrary power. He adds at this point that the body exercising the legislative power may not transfer this power to another body or person.[62]

The limitation on government from Locke's theory that has received the most attention is based on his statement that the "supreme power cannot take from any man any part of his property without his own consent...."[63] The tendency to interpret this statement as an absolute limit on the legislative power can, to some extent, be traced to Locke's earlier assertions that men entered civil society to provide better protection for their property. But it is quite possible for civil society to provide enhanced security for property without going to the extent of endowing the individual with an absolute right of ownership.[64] That Locke saw this

---

[57] Locke, *Civil Government*, ¶134, also 149, 150. The legislative power need not be housed in a legislature, for it is but the power to make law and could reside in a single person. *Ibid.*, ¶132. However, the whole thrust of Locke's argument is toward the predominating influence of the legislature.

[58] *Ibid.*, ¶149. See also the statement in the same section that "[t]he community perpetually retains a supreme power of saving themselves...."

[59] *Ibid.*, ¶135, 137, 142.

[60] *Ibid.*, ¶135.

[61] *Ibid.*, ¶137.

[62] *Ibid.*, ¶141.

[63] *Ibid.*, ¶138.

[64] Cf. Laslett, "Introduction," p. 116, n. 15.

protection as merely a protection against the arbitrary taking of property is apparent from his discussion of the legislative body's power to tax, which occurs as part of his general discussion of the protection of property. He says,

> ... 'tis fit everyone who enjoys his share of the protection should pay out of his estate his proportion for the maintenance of it. But still it must be with his own consent, i.e. the consent of the majority, giving it either by themselves or their representatives chosen by them; for if any shall claim a power to lay and levy taxes on the people by his own authority, and without such consent of the people, he thereby invades the fundamental law of property, and subverts the end of government....[65]

Of particular note in this quotation is Locke's equation of "his own consent" with "the consent of the majority." Given the context in which he was writing, it is understandable that Locke saw no need for a specific, substantive protection for property. As Laslett has noted, "[e]ven the minutest control of property by political authority can be reconciled with the doctrine of *Two Treatises*...."[66] If those electing the legislative power were men of property, that power could not be expected to pose any kind of serious threat to the institution of private property in society. Thus, nowhere in the *Second Treatise* does Locke propose limited government in a substantive policy sense; indeed, he appears to assume that government will be absolute as long as it is not arbitrary.[67]

In opposition to the foregoing argument, it might be urged that Locke's justification of revolution provided a broadly popular, egalitarian element in his thought.[68] Any straightforward reading of the *Second Treatise* should lead to the conclusion that Locke was arguing for a right to revolt. Here again, he puts his case in universal terms, using words such as "the people" without qualification. Nonetheless, careful examination of his argument indicates that it does not contradict the interpretation that has Locke assuming the dominance of the propertied classes.

At two points, the beginning of his discussion of the dissolution of government and the conclusion of that part of the *Second Treatise*, Locke was exceptionally careful to emphasize that removal or change of the government does not in itself result in the destruction of the community, or social structure.[69] This occurs, says Locke, only when a country is invaded and its inhabitants are cast on their own resources in a situation similar to that of the state of nature.[70] Even during a revolution the social

---

[65] Locke, *Civil Government*, ¶140.
[66] Laslett, "Introduction," p. 118.
[67] Locke, *Civil Government*, ¶22–23.
[68] See Julian H. Franklin, *John Locke and the Theory of Sovereignty* (Cambridge: Cambridge University Press, 1978), pp. 87–126, for later interpretations of Locke that saw his discussion of revolution as evidence that Locke was a political and social leveller.
[69] Locke, *Civil Government*, ¶211, 243.
[70] *Ibid.*, ¶211.

community will remain, and it was this set of relationships that was entered into by covenant for the better protection of property.[71] Furthermore, Locke does not seem to envision the possibility that the community itself, which would be dominated by the propertied, could abuse its power.

Although Locke's view of political authority is more broadly based than that of Hobbes—in that he allows for election of the legislature, supreme authority in the community, a right of revolution, and legislative dominance[72]—he is still speaking in terms of powerful governmental authority exercised by a small element of society. In some ways, the *Second Treatise* is not far removed from Locke's 1660 thoughts supporting an absolute magistrate. In the later work, Locke was not opposed to absolute governmental power; he *was* concerned about *arbitrary* absolute power. But as long as proper procedures were observed, Locke seemed satisfied that a government based on the participation of the propertied could be trusted to provide just leadership for the nation.

The democratic ramifications that have been developed from Locke's ideas were formulated in social contexts different from that of seventeenth-century England. Unfortunately, Locke left himself open to misinterpretation by casting his pronouncements in universal terms and by failing to articulate the conceptual bridges between stated ideas that now seem contradictory or confusing.[73] For the student of thought hoping for continued development of a theoretical basis for authority in the state, Locke's approach was disastrous.[74] His assumptions about the power of the propertied seem to have carried through most of the eighteenth century, but it was only natural that his written work should survive longer and should provide the basis for later interpretation. Thus, for students of political thought and ideologues, Locke's broad statements about individual rights completely overshadowed considerations of authority. It has been only recently, after serious damage to liberal thought has been inflicted, that scholars have utilized their knowledge of the seventeenth-century context to read Locke in a more accurate light.

Eighteenth-Century England: Judicial Authority and Ideological Consensus

My position has been that Locke definitely thought and wrote in terms of political control by the propertied, from his early unpublished statements of the need for an absolute magistrate through his position in the

---

[71] *Ibid.*, ¶222.
[72] The last point is to a certain degree a matter of a difference of emphasis in Locke and Hobbes.
[73] See Macpherson, *op. cit.*, p. 251; Laslett, "Introduction," p. 134.
[74] Cf. Laslett, "Introduction," p. 134.

Second Treatise granting supremacy to the legislative power. Certainly, English politics following Locke supports this interpretation. The eighteenth century has been seen by a variety of commentators as having been a period in which the propertied—landed gentry and wealthy merchants and financiers—controlled the politics of England. There was an element of real equality before the law for all classes in Augustan England, but the propertied's stance that it was their obligation to rule and the role of the propertyless to serve was essentially unchallenged during this period.[75]

In light of the problems posed by Locke's lack of theoretical thoroughness, it is ironical that the very ambiguity of his works on politics allowed them to serve for most of the succeeding century as guides for political action. England of the eighteenth century was a closed, hierarchical system dominated by those with property. Consensus on fundamental values among those involved in governing allowed much to go unsaid and unexamined. In this period, Locke's political thought could still be used and accepted for what it was intended to be—a justification for government by those of property for those of property.

The political history of England in the century following Locke's *Second Treatise* rather crassly reflected his assumptions about the propertied basis for political power. The primary source of legitimacy for governmental power appears to have been the values projected and supported by judicial enforcement of the law, a law which became increasingly harsh and protective of narrow economic interests as the century progressed. Yet despite the exploitative, oligarchical nature of English politics during this period, the eighteenth century was an era of remarkable political and social stability in England.[76] Locke remained the dominating influence, along with Newton, among intellectuals, but it was his *Essay Concerning Human Understanding*, not his political works, that served as the fount of ideas for philosophical discussion, the one arena of thought where significant changes did occur. In the realm of practical politics, the belief that the propertied alone should govern must have received fairly widespread acceptance, for the relative quiet of this century was achieved in the absence of a police force or a permanent standing army.[77]

The assumptions and values that dominated eighteenth-century English politics were so overwhelming because, at the fundamental level at

---

[75] Derek Jarrett, *England in the Age of Hogarth* (Frogmore, St. Albans: Paladin, 1976), pp. 13–14.

[76] P. S. Atiyah, *The Rise and Fall of Freedom of Contract* (Oxford: Clarendon Press, 1979), p. 23.

[77] Atiyah, *op. cit.*, p. 23; Douglas Hay, "Property, Authority and the Criminal Law" in Douglas Hay *et. al.*, *Albion's Fatal Tree* (New York: Pantheon Books, 1975), p. 18.

which they were operative, they existed unnoticed. The social cohesiveness of the classes ruling England in the eighteenth century has received the attention of several writers. Douglas Hay has estimated that no more than 3% of the population could participate in the political process. This group consisted of the monarchy and its relations, the aristocracy, the gentry, and some of the wealthiest merchants.[78] P. S. Atiyah describes the ruling segment as rather like a "property owners' association" in which most of the participants knew and interacted with each other socially as well as politically.[79] The control of a relatively developed nation by such a small portion of the population without the institutionalized forms of legalized force that are today regarded as essential to social stability suggests that even in the modern age there are social bases for authority that do not derive from the constructions posited by the formalistically oriented rationalists.

Although the English ruling classes of this period did not hesitate to act and to legislate to further their narrow economic interests, an important element of feudal traditional relationships remained as a part of their belief system. They saw their position as more than a means of material self-aggrandizement. For them, it carried with it an obligation to shoulder much of the cost of government and to provide for the poor and less fortunate.[80] The dominant-subordinate class relationships that composed the social fabric included intangible, yet real, forms of reciprocity of service.

A curious relationship which seems to have held for much of this period in England was that between the expanding power of the propertied, who moved rapidly to free their wealth from state and traditional encumbrances, and the creation of individual legal rights that applied throughout society. The Glorious Revolution of 1688 finally assured the dominance of the propertied classes for at least two centuries. Yet the struggle between Parliament and Crown was not definitively settled without the affirmation of important rights in the legal process that had been established during this period of instability. The independence of judges and non-accountability of juries, for example, were protections that were

---

[78] Hay, *op. cit.*, pp. 18, 61. It might be noted also that the newly rich, even though disenfranchised, could at times exercise considerable influence on government policy because of their power over the funding of the national debt. See Isaac Kramnick, *Bolingbroke and His Circle* (Cambridge, MA.: Harvard University Press, 1968), pp. 40–41.

[79] Atiyah, *op. cit.*, pp. 12, 21. This segment of society was not completely closed. The legal profession provided one route for able individuals from humble circumstances to rise socially. Others who acquired great wealth could purchase land and arrange to have themselves or their sons granted titles of nobility. See *ibid.*, p. 113; Kramnick, *op. cit.*, p. 50.

[80] Hay, *op. cit.*, p. 53; Kramnick, *op. cit.*, p. 55; Atiyah, *op. cit.*, pp. 77, 89–90.

seen as extending to all Englishmen, including the poorest in the realm.[81] E. P. Thompson argues that the rule of law established in the eighteenth century and derived from the conflicts of the seventeenth was "a true and important cultural achievement."[82] The result was that England, for its time, was one of the freest and most liberal countries in the world.[83] The propertied's use of law as an instrument for the protection of their economic interests at the same time reinforced the authority of the primary medium for the protection of the rights of the propertyless.[84]

The acceptance of the worth of property and of the natural leadership role of those who held property was also strongly encouraged by the ritual, what Hay terms the "majesty,"[85] of the judicial process. The law seems to have stood as the single most important legitimizing force of eighteenth-century England. In the words of Thompson, "the rhetoric of eighteenth-century England is saturated with the notion of law. . . ."[86] The judges of England were, of course, the paramount source of the law and the values that it was intended to inculcate, and, if Hay is to be believed, the judiciary took very seriously their role as propounders of the social values of the nation. The semi-annual visits of the courts of assizes to each of the counties were, in particular, the occasions for great public interest. In a statement that summarizes all the force of sovereign power, Hays describes the assizes as "coupled with wealth, a considered use of imagery, eloquent speech, and the power of death. . . ."[87] Here, then, was a reasonable facsimile of Hobbes's sovereign drawing on terror and propagation of correct doctrine as tools of power. The rhetoric of the law transmitted the interests of the propertied into the daily details of the lives of the common people in terms that were authoritative and often terrifying.

For the language of the law to be effective, the law itself had to produce believable results and, in its attention to the rights of all Englishmen, it did so. As Thompson has pointed out, the rhetoric of the law assumed a life of its own that eventually, with the waning of the political power of the traditional propertied interests, enveloped these very interests into a political system based on new sources of power.[88] The use of the law as applied by its judges for furtherance of economic interests, however, was to remain a part of liberal politics, particularly in the United States, where the interpretation of the Fourteenth Amendment was at times

---

[81] Atiyah, *op. cit.*, pp. 13–14.
[82] E. P. Thompson, *Whigs and Hunters* (New York: Pantheon Books, 1975), p. 265.
[83] Atiyah, *op. cit.*, pp. 14, 77; Sabine, *op. cit.*, p. 542; Jarrett, *op. cit.*, p. 14.
[84] Thompson, *op. cit.*, pp. 264–265.
[85] Hay, *op. cit.*, pp. 26–31.
[86] Thompson, *op. cit.*, p. 263.
[87] Hay, *op. cit.*, p. 27.
[88] Thompson, *op. cit.*, p. 269.

to resemble the civil equivalent of the pomp and ceremony of the eighteenth-century courts of assize.

Conclusions: Liberalism Moves Into the Nineteenth Century

Locke's reliance on unstated assumptions about the political importance of the propertied may have left the field open for Hobbes's view to serve as the basis for contemporary American arguments on who may legitimately participate in the political process. Locke saw the propertied as having a greater stake in government than the laboring classes. But additionally he seems to have seen them as more rational than the unpropertied, and, in this respect, they were also more qualified to govern. Hobbes, on the other hand, fairly clearly took the position that the individual could judge his own interests best, although, of course, he was not advocating a suffrage based on this principle. It has been, nonetheless, Hobbes's view of individual capabilities that has survived and prospered in liberal thought, and it has been this position that has served as an important rationale for continued extension of the suffrage to the point where some now argue for allowing the mentally retarded to exercise the vote.[89]

Viewed from another perspective, liberalism's debt to the social context within which its concepts have been formulated can be seen as having its origins in the ideas of Locke and Hobbes. Clearly, Hobbes's attention to the development of powerful, scientifically respectable political authority reflected his fear of the social chaos of his time. Under the conditions of personal insecurity fostered by the English Civil War, his explicit recognition of the importance of governmental power to social stability is easily understandable. Locke's acceptance of powerful government was somewhat less wholehearted, and certainly less articulate, than that of Hobbes, and, in retrospect, this appears to have been due to Locke's recognition of the stabilizing effect of the increasing power of the propertied in England. The rudimentary constitutionalism that can be found in his thought can be traced fairly directly to his confidence in social stability, a confidence made explicit in his discussion of revolution. The liberal attachment to the concept of the rule of law received further support from the Englishmen of property throughout the eighteenth century, when the underlying social agreement allowed the judicial promulgation of the law to achieve a high level of acceptance.

With the social relationships dominated by the propertied taken as given, political thought atrophied. Hobbes's statement remained the only comprehensive modern treatment of the theoretical foundations of

---

[89] See Barbara B. Green and Nancy K. Klein, "The Mentally Retarded and the Right to Vote," *Polity*, XIII (Winter, 1980), 184–206.

strong political authority, but it was overshadowed by the appeal of Locke's thought, which assumed far more than it articulated with regard to political authority. It was the onset of the Industrial Revolution that occupied the minds of the citizens of the succeeding century, with entrepreneurs trying to increase their wealth and position and the landed gentry trying desperately to hold on to theirs. The dislocations caused by rapid industrialization and the political repercussions of the revolutions in America and France brought political thinking into some prominence again, although it continued to be subordinate to economic concerns. Comparison of two thinkers of this later period, Jeremy Bentham and Edmund Burke, provides instructive insight with regard to the inability of liberalism to construct a theoretical framework capable of encompassing a justification for effective governmental authority that was both democratically responsible and constitutionally bounded.

In many respects, the lives of Burke and Bentham reflect the failures of modern liberalism. Each, in his way, reacted to the corrosive effect that David Hume had had on the shibboleths of English political thought through the distinctions that he drew between reason, fact, and value. To a great extent, Bentham accepted Hume's distinctions and turned to the rational calculation of political good from the values of pleasure and pain. In contrast, Burke found these values too shallow for political life and attempted to circumvent Hume by combining reason, fact, and value in the experience of the English nation.

Bentham and Burke

THEORETICAL ALTERNATIVES TO GOVERNMENTAL AUTHORITY

After the stagnation in political ideas during most of the eighteenth century, the fifty years from approximately 1775 to 1825 witnessed the emergence of an important revision of liberalism in the form of Jeremy Bentham's utilitarianism and the articulation of the classic Anglo-American statement of traditional conservatism in the thought of Edmund Burke. Burke provided a clear statement of the value of traditional sources of legitimation for governmental authority and, in general, his ideas provide an important critique of the assumptions and conclusions of liberalism. But, although Burke's writings and speeches may have blunted the radical consequences of the French Revolution for England, they were not sufficiently persuasive to overcome the growing attraction of liberal ideas for his countrymen. Bentham, himself, may not have had a great impact on the governmental policy of his time, but, in examining his ideas, one is struck by the degree to which he presaged the development of scientific formalism in social thought, the turn to behavioral forms of social control to assure institutional efficiency, and the emergence of an interventionist state.

The arguments for laissez faire individualism that James Mill and later Herbert Spencer were to make appeared in their economic form in Bentham's *Defense of Usury*, but these ideas did not constitute an essential part of his utilitarianism. The overriding thrust of Bentham's reformist position was toward the rational implementation of change through governmental action. Bentham carried the belief in man's capacity to change society for the better further than had any previous liberal thinker, but his reliance on formalistic rational analysis as the basis for public policy carried within it the seeds of political disruption and discord. As he demonstrated with his early attack on Blackstone and the common law, his theoretical approach could have a devastating effect on accepted beliefs and practices, and, in fact, it was one of the influences that helped to destroy the traditional consensus that had seemed to hold the English nation together throughout the eighteenth century. However, the ultimate consequence of building on a foundation of formalistic or scientific rationality was the destruction of any viable source of national consensus for public policy or governmental action, a ramification that became increasingly obvious in twentieth-century America. In this regard, Bentham's personality is a clue to the future of liberalism as embodied in the interventionist state, for the man was a highly eccentric person and many of the schemes for social reform that he proposed in the cause of more rational social policy seemed peculiar at the time and appear to be even more so today. Bentham's ideas suggest that the bounds of what might be advocated under the rubric of "rational public policy" can be very broad indeed and that a government operating under the criterion of Benthamite rationality would find itself on highly unsteady grounds. Nonetheless, the claims of positivistic rationality and of science have always had a tremendous appeal for liberal thinkers and, since they have been enlisted in the cause of active government, the proposals made in their name have probably exceeded the ruminations of even Bentham.

The rise to importance of the arguments for laissez faire effectively countered Bentham's arguments for powerful government and diluted his immediate influence on public policy. Bentham remains exceptionally important, however, for tracing the evolution of liberalism's views on governmental authority because his suggestions on control of human behavior, in many respects, became unarticulated social policy and thus eliminated the need for many liberals to support strong, directive government. Thus, while laissez faire liberals were arguing for enhancement of individual freedom through limits on government, they were diligently cultivating other forms of social control that had been suggested in Bentham's thought.

The alternative statements of the position of governmental authority provided by Bentham and Burke were responses to a wide range of social, economic, political, and philosophical developments that, by the close of the eighteenth century, demanded philosophical framing. Industrial development was rapidly refashioning social and economic relationships, and these changes engendered abuses and maladjustments that became increasingly pressing in the public mind. Equally pressing, from the point of view of those in political power and those with substantial property, were the ideological forces that had gained ascendency in America and France as the result of revolution. Finally, the analytical effects of David Hume's ideas had seriously weakened the old belief systems. Such Lockean staples as natural rights and contract theory could no longer serve as the bases for political action or belief when their relevance had been so clearly undermined by changing conditions and their philosophical validity had been destroyed by Hume.

After David Hume's treatment of it in the eighteenth century, use of the term "reason" as a standard of validity in political philosophy changed dramatically. Hume divided previous uses of reason into three categories.[1] Earlier thinkers, he asserted, had failed to distinguish between abstract logical relationships, the experience of observed events such as those described as "cause and effect," and moral truths that were really nothing more than practices that men generally deemed to be good. All of the foregoing relationships had been viewed indiscriminately and erroneously as the dictates of reason governing human existence. Hume argued that accurate use of the term "reason" occurred only when it was applied to the category of abstract, logical relationships. Here, premises, conclusions, and their necessary derivations proceeded according to rules that provided definite, particular, and predictable results. This area of knowledge was self-contained, as in mathematics, and it had no necessary relationship to real world facts or experiences. Indeed, events in the real world did not follow the dictates of reason, because they lacked the precision and certainty of purely rational relationships. Cause and effect, for example, are not joined by a necessary relationship but merely describe events that experience has taught occur sequentially with a high degree of frequency. "Reason can never shew us the connexion of one object with another, tho' aided by experience, and the observation of their constant conjunction in all past instances...."[2] Finally, natural law ideas simply reflected an attachment to conventions that men had found to be beneficial. With these distinctions, Hume destroyed the logical and scientific viability of those political beliefs and practices that liberals had cloaked with the claims of reason.

Hume's clarification of the concept of the rational did not prevent later use and abuse of the idea in political thought. But his examination of it did force later thinkers to use the idea differently. Bentham, for example, tried to remain within the Humean paradigm by constructing a highly formalized system that became artificial and subjective in its elaboration and application. Burke, on the other hand, rejected Hume's distinction between reason, fact, and value as too artificial for political life, and he circumvented the issue by combining the concepts.[3] For Burke, the political realities of England were the culmination of centuries of wisdom and were to be valued as good because of their roots in tradition, custom, and experience.

---

[1] This discussion draws heavily on Sabine, *op. cit.*, pp. 598–601.
[2] David Hume, *A Treatise of Human Nature.* Edited by L. A. Selby-Bigge (Oxford: Clarendon Press, 1973 [First published in 1739]), p. 92.
[3] Sabine, *op. cit.*, pp. 605–606.

As a liberal, Bentham spoke for reform and change; as a conservative, Burke defended the continuing value of the traditional political institutions of England. Bentham grounded his thought on a structure of formal reasoning that used individual psychology as its standard for governmental implementation of social reconstruction, and, in his faith in the capacity of the human intellect, he reflected an enduring element in liberal thought. Burke, on the other hand, had much less faith in the power of human intelligence, did not see social reconstruction as a primary goal of governmental policy, and did not fit in the liberal tradition. Neither thinker can be said to have had significant immediate influence, through their ideas, on the course of events in either England or the United States. Their theoretical statements are important, nonetheless, for the history of ideas and for the clarity with which they stated the opposing positions that were to remain important elements in the Anglo-American intellectual tradition.

Bentham: Liberal Ego and Latent Totalitarianism

In important respects, Bentham's political ideas reflected his tremendous ego and his peculiar and frenetic personality. Generally regarded as exceptionally intelligent, Bentham, it seems, awed even himself when he contemplated the level of genius with which he had been endowed.[4] James Steintrager reports that he may have seen himself as the Newton of the moral and social world.[5] He was, of course, known for his constant tinkering with all sorts of inventions, and this tinkering spirit appears as well in his approaches to social problems.[6] Bentham seems never to have matured into the seriousness that one normally associates with adulthood, but, as depicted by John Stuart Mill, functioned in a state of perpetual boyishness that was often characterized by a juvenile kind of pettiness and enthusiasm for new projects.[7] In his old age, he became

---

[4] Nancy L. Rosenblum, *Bentham's Theory of the Modern State* (Cambridge, MA.: Harvard University Press, 1978), pp. 14–15.

[5] James Steintrager, *Bentham* (Ithaca, N.Y.: Cornell University Press, 1977), pp. 12–13.

[6] See Shirley Letwin, *The Pursuit of Certainty* (Cambridge: University Press, 1965), pp. 176–182 for discussion of Bentham as a gadgeteer. Bentham was unwilling even to allow his corpse to decompose in peace, for in his will he provided the bizarre stipulation that his estate would go to the University of London only if his body were stuffed and kept on display at the University. Apparently the financial straits of private universities were as dire then as they are now, for Bentham's stuffed cadaver remains at the University of London. George E. G. Catlin, *The Story of the Political Philosophers* (New York: McGraw-Hill, 1939), p. 358. A photograph of Bentham's stuffed personage can be found on page 72 of Leonard Broom and Philip Selznick, *Sociology* (Third edition; New York: Harper and Row, 1963).

[7] John Stuart Mill, *Dissertations and Discussions* (New York: Haskell House Publishers, 1973 [First published 1859]), vol. 1, pp. 354–355, 392, n.

increasingly dogmatic and cantankerous, turning against many of his close associates and disciples.[8] Many great thinkers have, of course, had idiosyncrasies of one sort or another, but of those commonly considered sane, Bentham clearly stands out as one of the more eccentric.[9]

In his disdain for history, aesthetics, and previous thinkers, Bentham represented a disturbing kind of tunnel-visioned egoism that is not far removed from the self-assurance of contemporary radicals and ideologues.[10] Although the values that he propounded included those of tolerance, justice, and pleasure,[11] Bentham was not concerned with human beings from a genuine sense of humaneness. His goal was one of efficiency in the state, and there are indications, to be treated at greater length below, that any conception of human dignity that he may have had remained subordinate to this goal. In the words of one who knew him and his ideas well, "no one, probably, who, in a highly instructed age, ever attempted to give a rule to all human conduct, set out with a more limited conception either of the agencies by which human conduct *is*, or of those by which it *should* be, influenced."[12] Given his estimate of himself and his interest in legislation, it was only natural that Bentham should have wished to hold public office.[13] Fortunately for the common Englishman, Bentham never obtained any practical political experience, and the one scheme of his that came close to fruition, prison reform, was finally buried by Parliament, much to his chagrin. Bentham, thus, remains in a rather tragic sense a singularly one-sided thinker, one who really had no comprehensive sense of the human condition and appears to have been incapable of sympathizing with his fellow beings. Secure in his opinion of the supremacy of his intellect, Bentham cast aside the cautions provided by the wisdom of experience and, for the most part, rejected the possibility that he could learn much from other thinkers.[14] Hobbes, to be sure, had proposed a highly authoritarian system in the pursuit of peace and security, but he did not suggest nor does it appear that he could have conceived of the detailed intervention into human lives that Bentham's personality and reform projects suggest.

---

[8] Steintrager, *op. cit.*, p. 94; Rosenblum, *op. cit.*, p. 25.

[9] One of Bentham's biographers states that, by the early 1800s, "the eccentricity of mind and personality was unmistakeable." Charles Warren Everett, *The Education of Jeremy Bentham* (New York: Columbia University Press, 1931), p. xix. For additional glimpses of Bentham's character, see: Catlin, *op. cit.*, pp. 356–359; Leslie Stephen, *The English Utilitarians* (London: University of London, 1950 [First published in 1900]), vol. 1, pp. 230–233.

[10] On Bentham's limitations in this respect, see Steintrager, *op. cit.*, p. 145; Rosenblum, *op. cit.*, p. 10; Mill, *op. cit.*, pp. 350–351.

[11] See Rosenblum's discussion, *op. cit.*, p. 152.

[12] J. S. Mill, *op. cit.*, p. 355.

[13] Rosenblum, *op. cit.*, p. 11.

[14] Rosenblum at *ibid.*, p. 29 notes Bentham's respect for Helvetius's ideas.

For Bentham, the basis of morality and the standard for public policy was that of utility.

> ...By the principle of utility is meant that principle which approves or disapproves of every action whatsoever, according to the tendency which it appears to have to augment or diminish the happiness of the party whose interest is in question...I say of every action whatsoever; and therefore not only of every action of a private individual, but of every measure of government.[15]

Each individual, Bentham asserted, is governed by the "two sovereign masters, *pain* and *pleasure*."[16] By establishing utility as the criterion for government policy and using this standard as the framework for rigorous logical analysis of social relations and governmental policy,[17] Bentham believed that he could eliminate erroneous and emotional hindrances to efficient government action. In Gertrude Himmelfarb's words, his values were those of "rationality, universality, simplicity, and consistency."[18]

The work that first brought Bentham to the attention of the English public was his searing critical analysis of Blackstone's exposition of the principles of the common law. Published anonymously, *A Fragment on Government* was an attempt to expose the illogical elements of the common law that had resulted from reliance on past authorities and acceptance of an approach that made the law a changing, unpredictable form of social regulation.[19] Bentham, Shirley Letwin argues, "was certain of having discovered the key to perfection, to a system of law that would need but minor correction once in a hundred years."[20] For the founder of utilitarianism, the concrete, lived experiences of the myriad variety of individuals composing society succumbed uniformly to the requirements of formal calculations based on the universal principle of utility.[21] The foibles of real people that were imprinted on the common law and its method were simply beyond the bounds of defensible rationality as Bentham saw it.

In his opposition to the forces of the status quo, Bentham continued the liberal tradition of advocacy of reform and change. As Nancy Rosen-

---

[15] Jeremy Bentham, *An Introduction to the Principles of Morals and Legislation* in Jeremy Bentham, *A Fragment on Government* [1776] and *An Introduction to the Principles of Morals and Legislation* [1789]. Edited with introduction by Wilfrid Harrison (Oxford: Basil Blackwell, 1948), p. 126.

[16] *Ibid.*, p. 127.

[17] Rosenblum, *op. cit.*, p. 22.

[18] Gertrude Himmelfarb, *Victorian Minds* (New York: Alfred A. Knopf, 1968), p. 78.

[19] Steintrager, *op. cit.*, p. 12; Letwin, *op. cit.*, p. 7. Everett, *op. cit.*, pp. 96–98 notes that the question of authorship helped initially to create much more notice than *A Fragment* would have otherwise received.

[20] Letwin, *op. cit.*, p. 6.

[21] See Bentham, *op. cit.*, pp. 151–153.

blum has pointed out, Bentham's use of individual psychology as the source of values and as the criterion for change provided him with a particularly effective weapon against the controlling ideologies of his time,[22] and, in this regard, his thought illustrates one facet of the liberating effects produced by Locke's *Essay Concerning Human Understanding*. Bentham's reliance on individual feelings was egalitarian in that he was clear that each individual must be considered as an equal unit of pleasure and pain relative to every other individual.[23] Political democracy was not, however, a logically necessary part of Bentham's theoretical system. He seems never to have thought that the judgments of individual citizens should enter into the decisions of public officials.[24] Calculations of pleasure and pain did not require granting status or validity to the judgments or intellect of the common person. In fact, during the greater part of his life, Bentham looked to the aristocracy and the monarchy as the best vehicles for effecting his many schemes for reform.[25]

Of the various ideas that Bentham tirelessly spewed forth, his panopticon proposal for penal reform provides a window to his character and indicates the ominous potential for the individual that his penchant for utilitarian social tinkering could have. In the presentation of his panopticon penal system, Bentham demonstrated, beyond a shadow of a doubt, the totalitarian nature of his utilitarianism. Derek Jarrett expresses a similar sentiment in his conclusion that "[w]hile other moralists sought a controlled society, Bentham offered something even better: a conditioned society."[26] As the name suggests, the panopticon was to be constructed so that the behavior of each prisoner would be subject to observation by the guards at all times.[27] In his original plans, Bentham provided that each prisoner would serve his entire prison sentence in total isolation from other prisoners, but, perhaps because of cost considerations, his later versions were more lenient in this respect.[28] Bentham's goal was to remold the prisoner into a socially useful being by subjecting him or her to continual observation and supervision. It might not be possible, he acknowledged, to watch everyone all of the time, but the important component of the system was to instill in the prisoners the belief that they were under continual observation. Additionally, Bentham would have permitted, indeed would have encouraged, public viewings of the prisoners.[29] Finally, even after release from prison, individuals

---

[22] Rosenblum, *op. cit.*, pp. 128–129.
[23] Atiyah, *op. cit.*, p. 340.
[24] See Rosenblum, *op. cit.*, pp. 146–147.
[25] See Atiyah, *op. cit.*, pp. 342–343.
[26] Jarrett, *op. cit.*, p. 102.
[27] Himmelfarb, *op. cit.*, p. 35.
[28] *Ibid.*, pp. 36, 45.
[29] *Ibid.*, p. 49.

were required to meet very stringent standards of behavior under the close supervision of the authorities.[30]

It may be that some would agree with Bentham that criminals should be treated harshly and that, in this view, panopticon may not appear to be a serious threat to individuals generally. But a person of Bentham's intellect and personality could not be confined to reforming prisoners alone. Bentham saw the panopticon as a model for dealing with individuals in a variety of social settings, including schools, factories, workhouses, and hospitals,[31] and seems to have been particularly interested in extending the panopticon system to the unemployed poor.[32] Rosenblum admits that Bentham saw the aforementioned institutions as places where his panopticon model could be suitably applied to refashion human behavior but argues that he did not see it as appropriate for social relationships generally.[33] These institutions taken in conjunction with Bentham's virulent anti-religiosity, however, appear to leave the family as one of the few important social institutions that fell outside of his reforming interest, and it is difficult to see a confirmed bachelor such as Bentham hesitating for very long to improve family relations as well.[34] Bentham's schemes for the betterment of mankind were not based on empathetic concern for the position of the common individual but on rational calculation of what was consistent in terms of utilitarian public policy. Thus, his attachment to the panopticon model of social control survived his conversion to representative democracy as the most desirable form of government.[35]

Additional light has been cast on Bentham's role as the founder of utilitarianism by Himmelfarb's suggestion that Bentham saw panopticon as an important opportunity for financial gain. With his proposal, Bentham may have been operating from basic capitalistic motives as well as those of a reformist hue, although he could well have seen the two as compatible. He seems to have believed that he would become the supervisor of the penal institution and that he would eventually be able to extend his authority over the unemployed poor as well. In his proposal to the government, he had provided that, as supervisor, he would be able to use the inmates as laborers in manufacturing endeavors. Bentham

---

[30] *Ibid.*, p. 57.

[31] *Ibid.*, p. 34; Steintrager, *op. cit.*, p. 80; Rosenblum, *op. cit.*, p. 19; Jarrett, *op. cit.*, p. 101.

[32] Himmelfarb, *op. cit.*, p. 71.

[33] Rosenblum, *op. cit.*, pp. 19–20.

[34] In fact Bentham's tinkering extended even to the playground, where, for example, he thought that young children might perform useful work if the see-saw could be connected as a power source to machinery. See Jarrett, *loc. cit.*

[35] See Himmelfarb, *op. cit.*, pp. 73–75.

purchased land for construction of a panopticon and endeavored for years to have Parliament and the King grant him the authority and the funds to implement the plan.[36] He was outraged when his plans were finally rejected by Parliament, and he blamed the King for personally intervening to effect their defeat.[37] Probably it is not too much to suggest that the English disadvantaged, even today, should be thankful that the government of Bentham's time, unreformed though it was, had the good sense to spare the lower sorts the ravages of this early form of liberal social engineering.

Bentham's anger at the demise of his proposal for penal reform provides an interesting backdrop for his turn toward representative government. His treatment at the hands of Parliament looms larger in the liberal tradition than simply a personal defeat for one of the more significant liberal thinkers, because the timing of his switch to representative government suggests that this change may have been heavily influenced by his irritation at the existing government. Steintrager asserts outright that the charge that Bentham became a democrat in his pique at the King for killing the panopticon plan is "almost certainly wrong."[38] He argues, and Elie Halevy seems to agree, that Bentham's motives must have been more complex and that a large share of the credit for his change of heart must be assigned to the influence of his budding friendship with James Mill.[39] Nonetheless, if Bentham is to be viewed as a whole person, and not simply as a mental automaton churning out reams and reams of scribbling, then the tremendous amount of time and effort that he put into the panopticon plan and his vindictive, childish nature have to be accorded their due influence on his life and thought at this time. The emotional, excessive, and embarrassing outbursts against the government and in support of representative government that occurred in his writings after his change of mind can not be unrelated to the degree of personal involvement that Bentham had in this portion of his theoretical system.[40]

The one point about Bentham's switch in allegiance to representative government that does receive general agreement is that the move did not weaken his support for strong government. In this conversion, the source of political power was transferred to the people, but the power

---

[36] *Ibid.*, pp. 58, 62, 66–67, 71; Steintrager, *op. cit.*, p. 80.

[37] See his statement, "[b]ut for him [the King], all the paupers in the country, would have been in my hands" quoted in Himmelfarb, *op. cit.*, p. 75.

[38] Steintrager, *op. cit.*, p. 82.

[39] *Ibid.*; Elie Halevy, *The Growth of Philosophical Radicalism* (Boston: Beacon Press, 1955 [First published in French in 1904]), pp. 251–259. But see also the comments of William Wilberforce in Stephen, *op. cit.*, p. 206.

[40] See Steintrager, *op. cit.*, p. 58.

itself continued to be exercised through potent government officials.[41] Rosenblum agrees that throughout his life, where government power was concerned, Bentham remained an absolutist, but she argues that his other values precluded his supporting a "strong state" in the modern sense.[42] There are, however, no guarantees for individual rights in Bentham's thought.[43] His support of economic laissez faire in the *Defense of Usury* rested on his interpretation of its utility, not on any inherent attachment to laissez faire as a value per se.[44] Throughout Bentham's thought, the standard of government action is defined by the calculation of its utility in producing pleasure and security.[45] If individual freedom had to be curtailed in order to further utilitarian values, then such action was by definition within the power of the government. Still, it might be noted that, while no guaranteed rights existed in Bentham's system, his application of the pleasure-pain calculus to government policy did result in his acceptance of a wide range of what might be labelled "consensual perversions," including many of the "victimless crimes" of today.[46]

Bentham's statements about the rationality of men can easily be misinterpreted, for, even after his move to representative government, he continued to view the masses as the raw materials of social experimentation directed by government officials with expertise in such matters.[47] As Steintrager notes, Bentham's assertion that men can be expected to act rationally if they can clearly see their best interests is a tautological position.[48] In reading through much of the voluminous manuscript material left by Bentham, he has located but one example given by Bentham of a situation where men could be expected to act rationally. Even in this example, that of a contract between two men, Bentham qualified the degree of rational calculation that could be anticipated.[49] Bentham's arguments for representative government stemmed from his fear of the corrupting influence of self-interest on public officials,[50] a concern no doubt reinforced by what he regarded as his shabby treatment at the hands of England's rulers. The efficient utilitarian state, Bentham emphasized, needed legislators and administrators with professional expertise.

---

[41] See Himmelfarb, *op. cit.*, p. 75; Bentham, *op. cit.*, pp. 125–126.

[42] Rosenblum, *op. cit.*, pp. 151–152.

[43] Amy Gutmann, *Liberal Equality* (Cambridge: Cambridge University Press, 1980), pp. 26–27. Atiyah, *op. cit.*, p. 328.

[44] Gutmann, *op. cit.*, p. 27.

[45] On the status of security as a value in Bentham's system, see Rosenblum, *op. cit.*, p. 53.

[46] Steintrager, *op. cit.*, pp. 30, 124; Atiyah, *op. cit.*, p. 340.

[47] Steintrager, *op. cit.*, pp. 98, 121; Himmelfarb, *op. cit.*, pp. 40, 75–76.

[48] Steintrager, *op. cit.*, pp. 16–17.

[49] *Ibid.*, p. 17.

[50] *Ibid.*, pp. 118, 197.

The people could select and remove their representatives, but they should have little input into the policy process itself.[51]

Despite the fact that he anticipated the bureaucratic state and was a prolific writer and tireless advocate of reform, there remains considerable controversy over whether Bentham had much influence on the English political reforms of the nineteenth century. Wilfrid Harrison asserts that for half a century after his death, "Benthamism" was the driving force for reform in England.[52] Steintrager sees Bentham's ideas as having "profoundly altered the course of English politics during the nineteenth century."[53] However, Leslie Stephen noted that "there is comparatively little mention of Bentham in contemporary memoirs...."[54] Others have suggested that utilitarianism may not have been an important force behind the major reforms of the nineteenth century.[55] Currin Shields states specifically that the Utilitarians opposed those reforms aimed at improving the political position of the working classes.[56] Rosenblum also refers to the debate over Bentham's influence and cites a number of journal articles in the late 1950s and in the 1960s that have contributed to this controversy.[57]

Whatever his immediate impact, Bentham provided one of the clearest and most thorough statements of the belief that man can solve social problems through the conscious application of reason implemented through governmental action.[58] In a sense, his ideas fill in the details of the ominous side of Hobbes. Hobbes spoke in general terms about the role of government in controlling society; Bentham filled in the specifics over a wide range of social relationships and moved toward a society of conditioned individuals. Bentham clearly understood the need for effective political authority and provided a rather simple theoretical rationale for the exercise of political power. There are, of course, many questions that can be raised about Bentham's thought, but one of the most basic must concern his claim that his theoretical system was based on rational analysis of the individual and his place in society. Bentham's reasoning was the formalistic, artificial logic of a mind detached, to a large degree, from the real experiences lived by the great majority of individuals and, as such, it was not rational in any workable social or

---

[51] Rosenblum, *op. cit.*, pp. 143–148.

[52] Wilfrid Harrison, "Introduction" in Bentham, *op. cit.*, p. xii.

[53] Steintrager, *op. cit.*, p. 11.

[54] Stephen, *op. cit.*, p. 169, n. 1.

[55] Atiyah, *op. cit.*, p. 371; Himmelfarb, *op. cit.*, p. 81.

[56] Currin Shields, "Introduction" in James Mill, *Representative Government*. Edited with introduction by Currin Shields (Indianapolis: Bobbs-Merrill, 1955 [First published in 1820]), p. 37.

[57] Rosenblum, *op. cit.*, p. 164, n. 4.

[58] See Atiyah, *op. cit.*, p. 326.

political sense. Because social relationships failed the demands of Bentham's logic in ubiquitous fashion, the whole field of human endeavor became his workshop. Unencumbered by the wisdom of human experience and the perspectives of real human beings, he rather easily transformed individuals into mere abstract units of formalistic calculations.[59] A government operating from such an orientation is hardly a pleasant prospect no matter how efficient it might be, and, understandably, practical politicians would shy away from such a stance. At the same time, Bentham's functional perspective and his conditioning approach to those at the mercy of social institutions foreshadowed forms of social control that were necessitated by an economy that rejected interventionist government yet required disciplined human beings in large numbers.[60]

James Mill: Disciple and Modifier

As Bentham's leading disciple and the moving force behind utilitarianism as a political effort, James Mill made important modifications in Bentham's ideas. Some of these changes stemmed from the need to summarize and organize the rambling commentaries of the master into a form that had popular appeal and could provide a coherent ideological basis for action. Of at least equal importance was Mill's integration of the ideas of classical economics, particularly those of David Ricardo, with the elements of Bentham's thought.[61] With this fusion, the possibilities for powerful government latent in Bentham's thought were shunted aside in favor of individualism, for Mill's statements for laissez faire tended to be both simplistic and unequivocal.[62]

Underlying Mill's declarations favoring individual freedom from governmental interference were definite notions about who should be allowed to govern. Again in the development of liberal thought, one discovers assumptions about the sources of political power serving as the inarticulate background for broad statements advocating individual freedom. Mill's educational upbringing was that of the Scottish kirk and, in contrast to the virulent anti-religious position of Bentham, there remained a strong Calvinist element in his thought.[63] In secular terms, Mill's Calvinism caused him to value individual sacrifice and hard work as

---

[59] "By ruthlessly ignoring the refractions of ideas and emotions, he [Bentham] produced devices of monstrous efficiency that left no room for humanity...." Letwin, *op. cit.*, p. 188.

[60] In the words of Michel Foucault, "Bentham is one of the most exemplary inventors of technologies of power." Michel Foucault, *Power/Knowledge*. Edited by Colin Gordon (New York: Pantheon Books, 1980), p. 156.

[61] Atiyah, *op. cit.*, pp. 310–311; Shields, *op. cit.*, pp. 16–17.

[62] Atiyah, *op. cit.*, p. 312.

[63] See Letwin, *op. cit.*, pp. 193, 198, 201–202.

important components of individual worth and to measure a person's worth by his or her achievements.

The emphasis on individual self-discipline became part of utilitarian doctrine at a time when this attribute was increasingly seen as essential to the development of economic prosperity and as a social virtue generally. In the area of sex and the family, Thomas Malthus had raised fears about population growth that made late marriage and birth control seem to be more important.[64] Self-discipline among the workers became of much greater importance to industry, where larger factories required a work force that was punctual and conscientious in performing tasks that were often characterized by drudgery, danger, and exertion. Similarly, in the business world, the use of contracts relatively free from government interference or amelioration left the parties involved dependent on their own resources for fulfillment of the obligations created. Letwin states that by the 1820s the personalized, informal world that Bentham had known most of his life was rapidly being displaced by the world of professional administration guided by the standard of efficiency.[65] In his discussion of Bentham, Michel Foucault makes the same point from a different perspective.

> ... [E]ven in such a highly developed administration as the French monarchy [there] were ... loopholes. It was a discontinuous, rambling, global system with little hold on detail. ... But the economic changes of the eighteenth century made it necessary to ensure the circulation of effects of power ... to individuals themselves, to their bodies, their gestures and all their daily actions. ...[66]

The Utilitarians were not content to allow the masses to discover for themselves the virtues of self-discipline and industriousness. In this regard, Bentham's concern with the need to reconstitute behavior patterns in order to produce increased conformity and efficiency had been a harbinger of a general, although far less directive, trend in social arrangements. Speaking of the reformers of the last decades of the eighteenth century, Jarrett remarks that behind their "apparent concern for freedom there was a new and unprecedented interest in direction and regulation...."[67] Thus, it became exceptionally important to the Utilitarians that the masses be "educated" to know their "true" self-interests in this new, more impersonal society. For Bentham, education had been one means toward insuring obedience to a rational social morality and to the law.[68] But Mill, who assigned a much reduced role to government

---

[64] Atiyah, *op. cit.*, pp. 272–278.
[65] Letwin, *op. cit.*, p. 212.
[66] Foucault, *op. cit.*, pp. 151–152.
[67] Jarrett, *op. cit.*, p. 101.
[68] Atiyah, *op. cit.*, pp. 268–269.

direction of society, was more heavily dependent on education as a means for molding the proper habits and attitudes among the populace.[69] This approach may have been a less efficient form of control than direct government regulation, but Mill's fear of government oppression precluded him from even considering greater reliance on governmental authority.

Mill's support for representative democracy stemmed from his view of human nature but was not a reflection of his confidence in the masses. Because rulers were no exception to the basic, "boundless" drive to obtain power over others, representative government was necessary to provide checks on them.[70] Mill admitted that institutionalized checks on public officials could lessen the effectiveness of government, but he argued that if representatives proved to be less than competent, they could be removed. Without provision for removal of representatives, however, there was no easy remedy for the abuse of power that must inevitably occur in government.[71] Mill's distrust of public officials and his laissez faire economic proclivities engendered a support for weak government that diluted considerably the force of Bentham's sympathy for powerful, effective government and reinforced the individualistic elements in liberalism that were to be so important to Herbert Spencer and his American counterparts. Nonetheless, it is important to remember that other non-governmental forces of control were at work.[72]

In Mill's view, representative government provided a means for dealing with man's baser instincts and was not a means for implementing egalitarian democratic assumptions. In fact, Mill had a very definite opinion as to which segment of society possessed the capability for effective political leadership. When he spoke of government instituting the greatest happiness for the greatest number, he intended that the terms of this phrase would be defined by the middle classes of England.[73] In his words, "[i]t is to be observed that the class which is universally described as both the most wise and the most virtuous part of the community, the middle rank, are wholly included in that part of the community which is not the aristocratical. . . ."[74] Representative government in the utilitarian mode was not to be in the least bit egalitarian; its function with regard to the masses was to represent their interests through the political power of the middle classes, who could be expected as well to act in the best

---

[69] Gutmann, op. cit., pp. 24–25; Letwin, op. cit., pp. 197–198.

[70] James Mill, op. cit., pp. 50, 54, 57, 67.

[71] Ibid., pp. 88–89; Gutmann, op. cit., p. 25.

[72] This latter point is one of the important insights of Foucault, who has rightly stated that the idea of power is "impoverished" if it is thought of solely in terms of governmental regulation. Foucault, op. cit., p. 158.

[73] Shields, op. cit., p. 34.

[74] James Mill, op. cit., p. 89.

interests of society as a whole.[75] Mill believed that, with or without political power, the middle classes served as natural leaders for the lesser classes.

> ... [T]he opinions of that class of the people who are below the middle rank are formed, and their minds are directed by that intelligent, that virtuous rank who come the most immediately in contact with them, to whom they fly for advice and assistance in all their numerous difficulties, upon whom they feel an immediate and daily dependence in health and in sickness, in infancy and in old age; to whom their children look up as models for their imitation, whose opinions they hear daily repeated and account it their honor to adopt. . . .[76]

The middle classes were the opinion leaders of society and, if they were given political power, their natural position would simply be formalized. Thus, the franchise need be extended only to those who were most likely to act in the best interests of society, and these, Mill suggested, were males of forty years or older who held substantial property.[77]

In some respects, the relation of Mill's thought to Bentham's parallels that of Locke's thought to the ideas of Hobbes. In each instance, the earlier thinker granted broad authority to government and dealt abstractly with the issue of providing security and stability most efficiently. Both Hobbes and Bentham were followed by thinkers speaking for particular classes in society who had economic motives for objecting to the political status quo. Although Locke and Mill made statements for individual freedom generally, these were in fact claims of the propertied classes and middle classes respectively. In both cases, the thinkers' emphasis on individual liberty has tended to overshadow the fact that they saw government as closely controlled by a particular class. Historically, it might be suggested, Hobbes and Bentham served as philosophical ice breakers for the economic convoys that were to follow.

Much of the criticism of the Utilitarians has focused on their highly formalistic approach to social problems, an approach that tended to make them narrow and dogmatic in their positions. John Stuart Mill characterized the founder of the movement as a "one-eyed man,"[78] and James Mill's *Essay on Government* was immediately attacked by Thomas

---

[75] *Ibid.*, p. 82; Shields, *op. cit.*, p. 38, n. 1.

[76] James Mill, *op. cit.*, p. 90, see also p. 91.

[77] *Ibid,* p. 74; Shields, *op. cit.*, p. 38. In fairness to Mill, it should be noted that his franchise qualifications were considerably broader than those existing at the time he suggested them. There is also the possibility that he hoped to soften the political impact of his proposals by not asking for too much at once, although substantively his proposals are consistent with his remarks about the working and lower classes. For the view that Mill was really arguing for universal male suffrage, see John Clive, *Macaulay* (New York: Vintage Books, 1975), pp. 126–127.

[78] J. S. Mill, *op. cit.*, p. 357.

Macaulay as having all the appearance of having been written by some-
one with no knowledge of actual governments.[79] From the romanticist
perspective, Thomas Carlyle and Samuel Coleridge both criticized the
English philosophy of their day as being too narrowly concerned with
epistemological and cognitive questions and as being unable to formulate responses to the ultimate questions of the human condition.[80] Amy
Gutmann claims that James Mill's *a priori* inductiveness reflected the
inability of liberals to provide a clear deductive model of the state.[81]
Deductive models of the state cast in eschatological terms can, of course,
be overly rigid and dangerously destabilizing to society, but it is difficult to argue that the foundations for political authority in the modern
state need no more theoretical support than a hedonistic psychology
interpreted in its public policy manifestations by the professional or
better elements in society.

Burke: Authority Derived From the Reason of Experience

In most philosophical respects, Edmund Burke does not fit within the
liberal intellectual tradition. His response to the vast social and industrial changes occurring in England was a reassertion of the values of the
past. Tradition, for him, was the embodiment of the highest reason of the
nation. Man was simply deluding himself when he asserted the primacy
of the ideas of one or a few contemporary thinkers in dealing with social
problems.[82] Society was not an artificial aggregation of individuals but a
complex, organic community moved ultimately by divine will. Burke's
writings and speeches represent the last reasonably viable political statement for the traditional forces that liberalism and its accompanying
social changes were destroying.

In terms of both life experience and ideas, it would be difficult to
imagine a more dramatic contrast than that between Bentham and Burke.
Burke was first and foremost a man of practical politics. He served many
years in Parliament, knew the ways of English politics intimately, and was
one of the leading political spokesmen of his day. Bentham had no
practical political experience, had no sense of the art of political negotia-
tion and compromise, and seems, on occasion at least, to have paid little
attention to important political events that were occurring in immediate
proximity to him.[83] While Bentham's logically rigorous proposals for
reform lacked political sophistication, Burke's political ideas drew di-

---

[79] Atiyah, *op. cit.*, p. 311. Macaulay also objected to the Utilitarians' sparse,
"Euclidean," world-view. See Clive, *op. cit.*, pp. 129–130.

[80] Letwin, *op. cit.*, pp. 224–225.

[81] Gutmann, *op. cit.*, p. 23.

[82] Halevy, *op. cit.*, pp. 163–164 gives us an excellent short statement of Burke's
position on the value of experience, prejudice, and prescription.

[83] On the last point, see Letwin, *op. cit.*, p. 178.

rectly on his experience in politics and his knowledge of English constitutional tradition. Bentham may be categorized in the rationalist, analytic tradition philosophically, but Burke's thought would seem to be more deserving of the label "rational" if that term is to be used to describe ideas that have a relevant and tangible relationship to political reality.

Burke viewed the kind of *a priori* reasoning used by Bentham in his pursuit of social tinkering as metaphysical and dangerous. He asserted that a position could be metaphysically true but morally and politically false.[84] Thinkers such as the Utilitarians and the intellectual inciters of the French Revolution focused on the "shell and husk" of history. They had no sense of man's needs or limitations. In their ideological machinations, they falsified reality and misled men.[85] Political theory, if it is to be constructive, is not a matter of *a priori* assumptions imposed on a contrite and struggling populace; it must draw on man's experience and natural beliefs.[86] For the proper interpretation of the "spirit of our constitution and the policy" which attended the Revolution of 1688, one should look not to "the sermons of the Old Jewry and the after-dinner toasts of the Revolution Society." One should instead follow the methods of a modern political scientist or historian and examine the English histories, the records of the period, and the acts and journals of Parliament.[87] Similarly, when he argued the case for the constitutional position of the British monarch, Burke drew not on abstract logic but on the historical facts as shown by the documents relevant to the issue.[88]

Burke pointed out that experiments in the physical sciences proceed very carefully and deliberately. Certainly, he argued, political leaders should be no less circumspect in their dealing with the lives of human beings, who tend to be more complex than the inanimate objects of scientific research in the "hard" sciences.[89] In order to contribute to the improvement of mankind, social reform must proceed with caution and continue the accepted and valuable practices of the past.[90]

> ...Besides, the people of England well know that the idea of inheritance furnishes a sure principle of conservation and a sure principle of transmission, without at all excluding a principle of improvement.... Thus, by preserving the method of nature in the conduct of the state, in what we

---

[84] Russell Kirk, *The Conservative Mind* (Third revised edition; Chicago: Henry Regnery, 1960), p. 59.

[85] Edmund Burke, *Reflections on the Revolution in France.* Edited with introduction by Thomas H. D. Mahoney (Indianapolis: Bobbs-Merrill, 1955 [First published in 1790]), p. 163; Himmelfarb, *op. cit.*, p. 16.

[86] Burke, *op. cit.*, p. 69.

[87] See *ibid.*, p. 35.

[88] *Ibid.*, pp. 15ff.

[89] *Ibid.*, p. 197.

[90] *Ibid.*, pp. 196–198.

improve we are never wholly new; in what we retain we are never wholly obsolete....[91]

Burke was not opposed to change, but it is clear that, in his mind, the conditions for social change were as important as the substance of the change itself.

Russell Kirk, perhaps the leading American scholar on Burke and his thought, concludes that, as a whole, Burke's most significant accomplishment was the "definition of a principle of order."[92] For Burke, the natural order of society was one of aristocracy and hierarchy.[93] "Good order is the foundation of all good things. To be enabled to acquire, the people, without being servile, must be tractable and obedient. The magistrate must have his reverence, the laws their authority."[94] The common people had essential dignity in their position as Englishmen. For the "feebler minds," the force of sound prejudice provided guidance. These "untaught feelings" were an important source of social stability and, at the same time, contributed a wholesome moral content to the lives of the less fortunate.[95] Those on the upward move socially should retain "a sense of habitual dignity which prevents that upstart insolence almost inevitably adhering to and disgracing those who are the first acquirers of any distinction...."[96] Every individual was enmeshed in the manifold relationships and values of that complex entity constituting the nation, and social stability required that individual movement in this context be neither abrupt nor arbitrary.

Burke's conception of individual liberties was phrased in terms of individual dignity at the same time that it gave weight to the requirements of social stability. The liberty of an Englishman, he declared, was a "manly, moral, regulated liberty."[97] The idea of freedom as freedom from all restraints was ludicrous. Such a definition ascribed moral worth to the liberty of the escaped prisoner and lunatic running loose as well as to that of the law-abiding citizen.[98] The natural rights of Englishmen were those of equal justice, security in labor and property, enjoyment of the amenities of civilized institutions, and the benefits of order.[99] The exercise of these rights required that human proclivities must be controlled if they infringed disruptively on the social order. It is government's duty to preserve the proper balance between stability and liberty

---

[91] *Ibid.*, p. 38.
[92] Kirk, *Conservative Mind*, p. 75.
[93] *Ibid.*, p. 65.
[94] Burke, *op. cit.*, p. 287.
[95] *Ibid.*, pp. 98–99; Himmelfarb, *op. cit.*, p. 18.
[96] Burke, *op. cit.*, p. 39.
[97] *Ibid.*, p. 8.
[98] *Ibid.*
[99] The list is from Kirk, *Conservative Mind*, p. 63.

within society, and this is not accomplished through abstract formulation but through sound political judgment as to the needs of each generation.[100] Burke agreed with Bentham that government is an artificial construction. But, he argued, it was not the "contrivance" of a moment's thought nor an *a priori* emanation from the hyperactive intelligence of one individual. It is instead the repository of the political wisdom of centuries and constitutes a contract between the nation and its past and future as well as the present. Burke's oft-cited description of the social contract merits repeating here.

> Society is indeed a contract. Subordinate contracts for objects of mere occasional interest may be dissolved at pleasure—but the state ought not to be considered as nothing better than a partnership agreement in a trade of pepper and coffee, calico, or tobacco, or some other such low concern, to be taken up for a little temporary interest, and to be dissolved by the fancy of the parties....
> It is a partnership in all science; a partnership in all art; a partnership in every virtue and in all perfection. As the ends of such a partnership cannot be obtained in many generations, it becomes a partnership not only between those who are living, but between those who are living, those who are dead, and those who are to be born. Each contract of each particular state is but a clause in the great primeval contract of eternal society...[101]

This passage sums up Burke's view of social obligation and demonstrates his answer to Hume, who had dismantled the contract of Locke and Hobbes. Burke's contract combines reason, fact, and value. It is the human experience over all time "in every virtue and all perfection." Similarly, Burke turned to the experience of the nation as the source of legitimation for governmental authority. Governmental authority stemmed, in a very real sense, from the people's recognition of its importance, not from the minds of reformers possessed of grandiose plans for the improvement of mankind. Burke's position for governmental power rests on national consensus and, as such, provides protection against the destruction of social norms by the competition between those who endeavor to turn the current view of what is rational to their own ends.

Good government must, as Burke saw it, ensure social stability and yet protect the lower orders as well as the higher. He was candid in his treatment of the place of the "people" under such government. Government policy was not a matter of simple arithmetic, where each counts as one and mere calculation determines the result.[102] Burke's reading of traditional English government relationships convinced him that the "inferior minds" were entitled to have their interests considered in the

---

[100] Burke, *op. cit.*, pp. 9, 69.
[101] *Ibid.*, p. 110.
[102] *Ibid.*, pp. 55, 59.

making of policy.[103] But there would always be distinctions in ability among individuals, and those with greater virtue and wisdom should have the greater say in government. The policy process should be open, but those without the initial advantage of higher class status should have to prove their merit by overcoming the obstacles that a class stratified society presented.[104] The ideal attributes of a political leader, Burke believed, included benevolence, a willingness to persevere in the face of difficulty, and flexibility toward change when change was clearly needed.[105] Traditional leadership of this quality would inspire moderation on the part of the people,[106] and their attachment to tradition would in turn inhibit leadership excesses.[107] In Burke's aphorism, "[k]ings will be tyrants from policy when subjects are rebels from principle."[108]

There is, of course, no question that, by today's standards in England or the United States, the plight of the lower classes in Burke's England was harsh. Still, their position was better than that of their counterparts in most other European countries and significantly better than that of the lower classes in Ireland from whence Burke came. An important part of Burke's ideological position was his belief that a national community acting on the basis of traditional values was far more protective of individual freedoms and dignity than would be the case in a society constructed by intellectuals with little or no practical experience in politics and without regard for the past. In his view, the "rationalists" wanted to strip society of the "decent drapery of life" and leave the poor without those consolations of religion and belief that made their lots in life bearable.[109] Dissolving the community into atomistic individuals, bound by nothing or no one other than an abstract logic declaring the reasonableness of their position, would be particularly cruel to the poor and others of the unfortunate in society.[110] Such a society would be like post-revolutionary France, a "national gaming table" at which all would be forced to compete but where only a few would have the capacity for understanding and manipulating the rules.[111]

The fate of Burke's thought in the century and a half after he lived indicates the influence that cultural forces external to politics can have on the survival of political ideas. Burke strongly supported the basic

---

[103] *Ibid.*, p. 197–198.
[104] *Ibid.*, pp. 57, 59.
[105] *Ibid.*, p. 181.
[106] See Harvey C. Mansfield, Jr., *Statesmanship and Party Government* (Chicago: University of Chicago Press, 1965), p. 163.
[107] *Ibid.*, p. 158.
[108] Burke, *op. cit.*, p. 89.
[109] *Ibid.*, pp. 87, 187.
[110] *Ibid.*, pp. 110–111.
[111] *Ibid.*, pp. 226–229.

rights of Englishmen and human beings generally and saw these rights as limits on governments. Thus, he backed the American colonists in their struggle with the mother country and bitterly attacked Hastings for his misgovernance of India. Because his definition of individual rights drew on the English past, these rights were not further claims on the government but were sources of social stability. At the same time, Burke's thought utilized English tradition and custom to place government authority on a firm theoretical and constitutional foundation. Whatever their virtues, Burke's ideas were not destined to carry the day in either England or the United States, primarily because they did not speak to the developing nonpolitical cultural forces that were to serve as sources of validation for the legitimacy of political ideas. As a statement for the status quo, Burke's position could not provide the flexibility toward change and the freedom of action that the increasingly aggressive entrepreneurial classes demanded. Second, Burke simply was not concerned with the use of science as a source of social values at a time when scientific claims in the social, political, and economic areas were beginning to carry tremendous weight with both popular and educated opinion. In America, it was not Burke, or Bentham, but Herbert Spencer who was to obtain the rapt attention of the public with social scientific positions that rationalized individual economic endeavor at the same time that they rendered the state largely irrelevant as a constructive social force. In retrospect, however, it appears that the proponents of laissez faire owed acceptance of their ideas as much to the quiet social infiltration of practices of behavior control as they did to the persuasiveness of their claims of scientific or economic inevitability. Almost without notice, the traditional forms of social control so eloquently defended by Burke had been replaced by institutional and economic means of control that rested quietly but effectively at the base of laissez faire ideology.

Science as Social Ideology

THE CULTURAL CONSTRAINTS OF
POST-BELLUM AMERICA

Although their systems dealt rather thoroughly with the theoretical bases for political authority and its exercise, the ideas of Burke and Bentham were not destined to play a major role in the development of contemporary liberalism in America, to which our treatment now shifts. Twentieth-century American liberalism can be explained in most of its essentials in terms of the overarching influence of one set of ideas, those of social evolution. Quite probably, without the emergence of Herbert Spencer and Charles Darwin, the ideas of Bentham's disciples would have received more currency and more thorough treatment in American intellectual circles. Clearly, the laissez faire ideas of the Manchester, or classical, liberal economists have had continuing influence in American economics. The ideas of John Stuart Mill appeared to be gaining considerable attention when, after the Civil War, they ran into the irresistible force of the ideas of Darwin and Spencer.[1] Spencer offered Americans a combination of evolutionary science and individualism that meshed exceptionally well with the needs of post-Civil War culture. The use, by Spencer, of a scientific basis for his individualism enabled him to limit the state as a form of social control to a bare minimum of functions. The effects in terms of a theoretical framework for directive political authority were obviously disastrous. For both Burke and Bentham, governmental power was a resource to be used for social good; for Spencer and

---

[1] In his editing of J. S. Mill's *Principles of Political Economy* for use in American schools, J. Laurence Laughlin omitted Mill's chapters justifying government action and providing limits to laissez faire. Sidney Fine, *Laissez Faire and the General-Welfare State* (Ann Arbor, MI.: University of Michigan Press, 1969 [First published in 1956]), p. 57. See Bruce Kuklick, *The Rise of American Philosophy* (New Haven: Yale University Press, 1977), pp. 21, 24, 45 for the overwhelming effects of Darwin on America's philosophers.

many Americans in the latter nineteenth century, it was in most respects a hindrance to progressive social purposes.

Herbert Spencer: Individualism and the Demise of Government Authority

In reading Herbert Spencer's *Social Statics*, one is struck by how close Spencer came to formulating the concept of evolution.[2] Viewed from the twentieth century, his discussions of biological change seem to assume the arguments of Darwin's *Origin of Species*.[3] The latter work did not appear until 1859, however, nine years after the publication of *Social Statics*. Obviously, evolutionary ideas were an important part of the intellectual milieu of the 1850s. Although *Origin of Species* did not deal with man, its publication gave tremendous support to the scientific claims that Spencer had previously made in his efforts to apply biological principles to society. Spencer, himself, seized on this opportunity and, in his later works, drew on Darwin for additional support.[4] And it was in his later work that he coined the phrase "survival of the fittest," although the idea was clearly contained in his first major work.[5]

The relationship between Spencer's ideas and those of Darwin was to become blurred in the minds of their popular American audiences, not only because of similarities in their ideas but also because these ideas were disseminated in America at about the same time. Both *Social Statics* and *Origin of Species* became intellectually salient in America just after the Civil War and were to combine to work a revolution in the entire continuum of thought. Technically, it would be more precise to treat Spencerianism as separate from social Darwinism because Spencer's ideas predated Darwin and could stand without the scientific support that Darwin appeared to provide. In fact, late in life, Spencer expressed some unhappiness that he had tied his ideas so closely to Darwinian evolution.[6] Yet it is safe to conclude that, to the American mind in the

---

[2] Spencer himself was "vexed" that he had failed to work his ideas through to the concept of evolution. See Ferdinand Tönnies, *On Social Ideas and Ideologies.* Edited, translated, and annotated by E. G. Jacoby (New York: Harper and Row, 1974), p. 108, n. 23.

[3] See Herbert Spencer, *Social Statics* (New York: Robert Schalkenbach Foundation, 1970 [First published in 1850]), pp. 55–56, 372–373, 391–396. This is a reprint of the original edition of *Social Statics*, which Spencer did not revise until the 1890s.

[4] Robert C. Bannister, *Social Darwinism* (Philadelphia: Temple University Press, 1979), pp. 48–49, 50–56.

[5] Cf. *ibid.*, p. 45 and Cynthia Eagle Russett, *Darwin in America* (San Francisco: W. H. Freeman, 1976), p. 14 on the question of where Spencer first used the term.

[6] Ernest Albee, *A History of English Utilitarianism* (New York: Macmillan Company, 1957 [First published 1901]), p. 356.

post-war era, social Darwinism was a mixture of ideas that drew most heavily on Spencer with a tincture of extrapolation from Darwin's work.

There is no mistaking the popularity of Spencer's ideas during this period.[7] *Social Statics*, especially with the assistance from Darwinian sources, quite simply encompassed the fundamental ideological needs of articulate Americans of the period from 1865 to 1900. It provided the requisite grounding in science.[8] It assured Americans that their individualism was the route to progress.[9] Further, the atheistic possibilities of pure Darwinism could be avoided with Spencer's reliance on Divine will and its working through nature and his later postulation of an "Unknown Cause" in the universe.[10] Perhaps most important, businessmen could identify with an approach that proclaimed freedom of individual endeavor as the only route to human perfection.[11] They could wholeheartedly agree with Spencer's proclamation that

> ... [if a person] obtains, by his greater strength, greater ingenuity, or greater application, more gratifications and sources of gratification than ... [other persons], and does this without trenching upon the equal freedoms of the rest, the moral law assigns him an exclusive right to all those extra gratifications and sources of gratifications....[12]

It might also be noted here that Spencer's early opposition to private ownership of land was removed from the revised edition of *Social Statics*.

Given the dominance of the businessman in all areas of American life during the latter nineteenth century, Spencer's ideas were assured at least a fair hearing.[13] But, in fact, they appear to have appealed to many sectors of American society. Sidney Fine argues that Spencer was "deemed by many Americans to be the greatest thinker of the age."[14] He quotes John R. Commons's remark that he was "brought up on Hoosierism, Republicanism, Presbyterianism, and Spencerism" in Indiana and notes

---

[7] See Russett, *op. cit.*, pp. 16–17.

[8] See Bannister, *op. cit.*, p. 66 on the importance of social science in America by the mid-nineteenth century.

[9] "Progress, therefore, is not an accident, but a necessity. . . ." declared Spencer, *op. cit.*, p. 60.

[10] See Spencer, *op. cit.*, pp. 61, 68, 175; for mention of the "Unknown Cause," see Herbert Spencer, *The Study of Sociology* (New York: D. Appleton and Company, 1896 [First published in 1873], pp. 282–284; Herbert Spencer, *Social Statics, Abridged and Revised: Together with the Man Versus the State* (New York: D. Appleton and Company, 1896), p. 419. The revised edition contains fairly extensive changes in wording and will be differentiated from the original edition by the date 1896. Kuklick, *op. cit.*, p. 26 notes the role of the "Unknowable" in Spencer's thought.

[11] Spencer, *Social Statics*, p. 60.

[12] Spencer, *Social Statics* (1896), p. 66; cf. Spencer, *Social Statics*, p. 279.

[13] See Fine, *op. cit.*, pp. 30, 117.

[14] *Ibid.*, p. 41.

Commons's assertion that his father and all his father's friends were followers of Spencer.[15] For some of the reasons noted later in the discussion of English reform in the nineteenth century, Spencer's ideas never gained much currency in his native land.[16] But when he visited America in 1882, he was treated as a popular hero, and the famous banquet in his honor at Delmonico's was attended by the leading figures of the day.[17] Americans of the period believed that they had everything that they needed in Spencer's ideas—an optimistic, scientifically respectable, individualistic, and religiously viable statement of man's place in the cosmos.

In *Social Statics*, Spencer applied what he saw as the laws of biological development to the social sphere.[18] Morality was "a species of transcendental physiology."[19] All of nature displayed a progressive movement by organisms toward adaptation to their environments.[20] "The modifications mankind have undergone and are still undergoing result from a law underlying the whole organic creation; and provided the human race continues and the constitution of things remains the same, those modifications must end in completeness...."[21] "Thus the ultimate development of the ideal man is logically certain ..."[22] If man is to develop into a perfectly free and moral being, his adaptive processes must be allowed to operate freely. The first principle of "right social relationships" is that "[e]very man has freedom to do all that he wills, provided he infringes not the equal freedom of any other man. . . ."[23] Spencer was especially careful to point out, with regard to this principle, that those qualifications to liberty that allow for the equal freedom of others are voluntary.[24] The development of man's moral nature must be spontaneous for adaptation to work its will.[25] The state could not have a positive moral function if social evolution were to be allowed to continue.[26]

For Spencer, the state was a free association of individuals for their mutual protection.[27] It rested on the willing support of its citizens, and theoretically an individual had the right to adopt "a condition of vol-

---

[15] *Ibid.*, p. 42.
[16] *Ibid.*, p. 41, n. 27; also p. 61–62 below.
[17] Bannister, *op. cit.*, pp. 76–77; Richard Hofstadter, *Social Darwinism in American Thought* (Revised edition; Boston: Beacon Press, 1955), pp. 48–49.
[18] Spencer, *Social Statics*, p. 56.
[19] *Ibid.*, p. 391.
[20] *Ibid.*, pp. 55–56, 389.
[21] *Ibid.*, p. 60.
[22] *Ibid.*, p. 59.
[23] *Ibid.*, pp. 69, 95.
[24] *Ibid.*, p. 95.
[25] *Ibid.*, p. 64.
[26] *Ibid.*, p. 224.
[27] *Ibid.*, p. 246.

untary outlawry."[28] As soon as the state moved beyond its accepted functions of defense, police protection, and judicial decision-making, it invited dissent from those who did not agree with the additional functions.[29] More importantly, state provision of services interferes with the laws of nature. The state is wasteful and clumsy in its attempts to provide services. It threatens the delicate, complex fabric of society,[30] and at the same time denies the taxpayer the chance to develop his faculties fully through the use of his money.[31] The state is "doubly detrimental" to this individual because, in addition to taking his money, by providing services that he should be able to handle for himself, it deprives him of the opportunity to develop to the fullest his capacity to take care of himself.[32]

It was in his consideration of the justifiability of England's attempts to ameliorate the lot of the poor that Spencer made statements that still send shivers up the backs of welfare liberals. He did not shrink from the fact that his approach to government would leave some individuals at a terrible disadvantage. But the progress of mankind required that those who did not adapt well to the social conditions of an era must fall by the wayside. "Pervading all nature we may see at work a stern discipline, which is a little cruel that it may be very kind. . . ."[33] The biological laws governing the lower organisms apply in their harshness and ultimate reward to man as well. On this point, Spencer deserves quotation at some length.

> . . . The poverty of the incapable, the distresses that come upon the imprudent, the starvation of the idle, and those shoulderings aside of the weak by the strong, which leave so many "in shallows and in miseries" are the decrees of a large, far-seeing benevolence. It seems hard that an unskilfullness which with all his efforts he cannot overcome should entail hunger upon the artisan. It seems hard that a laborer incapacitated by sickness from competing with his stronger fellows should have to bear the resulting privations. It seems hard that widows and orphans should be left to struggle for life or death. Nevertheless, when regarded not separately, but in connection with the interests of universal humanity, these harsh fatalities are seen to be full of the highest beneficence—the same beneficence which brings to early graves the children of diseased parents and singles out the low-spirited, the intemperate, and the debilitated as the victims of an epidemic.[34]

---

[28] *Ibid.*, p. 185. Later in this section of *Social Statics*, Spencer cautioned that, practically speaking, the right to ignore the state without serious consequences was some time off. *Ibid.*, p. 194.

[29] *Ibid.*, pp. 227–249, *passim*, 253. See Fine, *op. cit.*, pp. 38–39 for a summary of the functions that Spencer would have removed from the state. Many of these are now seen as essential duties of the state.

[30] Spencer, *Study of Sociology*, pp. 11, 14, 19.

[31] Spencer, *Social Statics*, pp. 250, 261.

[32] *Ibid.*, p. 251.

[33] *Ibid.*, p. 288.

[34] *Ibid.*, p. 289; see also Spencer, *Study of Sociology*, p. 314.

Although he recognized that it would interfere with nature's way to some extent, Spencer did support voluntary charity because it would enhance the moral beneficence faculty of the giver.[35]

One can, of course, make many criticisms of Spencer's approach toward the improvement of mankind. Americans certainly did not follow his more extreme arguments for limited government, even though they were his most enthusiastic supporters and applied his ideas generally to the economic area. Spencer, however, was thinking in terms broader than mere material aggrandizement. To him, his proposals were pointed toward the realization of a truly moral race. He was disappointed in the ravages of industrialism in both England and America in his later years.[36]

Spencer's anti-statism has been a pervasive, continuing, and deleterious influence in American politics. In a very real sense, his ideas on the evil of governmental authority have undergirded the inability of Americans to come to grips with the issues relating to government authority. Inceptionally, his views encouraged the denigration of government. More serious, however, was the fact that attempts to implement reform in America had to answer Spencer's ideas first. In doing so, the reformers tended to be very wary of ideological absolutes of any kind and, thus, while arguing for governmentally instituted reform, were unable to provide an articulate, coherent value system for guiding such action. Their problems were further complicated by their continued optimism about human nature. Spencer was logically consistent on that point; without direction, man could be trusted to act morally over the long haul. The reformers did not disagree with man's innate goodness and rationality, but persisted in arguing that the masses needed governmental guidance.

Post-Bellum America: Liberalism Ensconced in Scientific Ideology

In America, the period following the Civil War was characterized by rapid economic and social change. The dissemination of technological advances impressed upon the popular mind the value of science in aiding man to control his environment.[37] These advances also engendered social changes that required direction and justification provided by a functional theoretical framework. The two major ideological positions contending for the American mind during the latter nineteenth

---

[35] Spencer, *Social Statics*, pp. 285, 291.

[36] "Intrinsically, a state in which our advance is measured by spread of manufactures and a concomitant production of such regions as the 'Black Country,' looking as though it had lately been invaded by an army of chimney-sweeps, is a state to be emerged from as quickly as possible...." Herbert Spencer, *Facts and Comments* (New York: D. Appleton and Company, 1902), pp. 7–8.

[37] Bert James Loewenberg, "Darwinism Comes to America, 1859–1900," *The Mississippi Valley Historical Review*, XXVIII (December, 1941), 359.

century both turned to claims of scientific legitimacy to validate their stands. Awed by the production and potential of industrialism, Americans were singularly unreceptive to philosophical positions with foundations outside a framework of scientific support. Through their proclaimed use of science, the intellectuals of the period seem to have overcome the practical-minded American's skepticism toward theorizing. At the same time, the exploitation of scientific claims and the scientific method in dealing with social relationships lessened the need for forthright examination and exposition of sources and purposes of governmental authority. For reformers, the experimental method could not validly proclaim particular social goals as true and, for the social Darwinists following Spencer's ideas, the evolutionary process operating inexorably in the social as well as biological world had no need of external direction.

The industrial northeast and the midwest provided the cultural sources for American thought for at least three-quarters of a century after the Civil War and, although this thought divided into two fairly distinct camps, it was liberal in its common fundamental assumptions. The area of the country with the economic and social traditions conducive to supporting a conservative alternative to the dominating post-bellum ideologies had been decimated by the war and by its attachment to slavery. The role that conservatism might have played, if it had attained a viable political status in post-war America, is suggested by the activities of the conservative forces in nineteenth-century England.

Due to Britain's feudal heritage, the British capitalist never received public homage to the degree that his American counterpart did. Even at the height of industrial expansion, the English landed interests retained sufficient prestige and political power to enable them to dilute the claims of the *nouveaux riches*.[38] Atiyah declares, without qualification, that laissez faire doctrine never was in ideological ascendancy among the governing classes and had no sustained influence on the direction of any specific government policy. Within this context, the conservatives of England were not at all reluctant to utilize governmental power to deal with social evils.[39] In their invocation of the state as an instrument for reforming the excesses of capitalism, they acted on the basis of beliefs

---

[38] In fact, the recently emergent industrial and financial magnates enhanced the position of the landed aristocracy by emulating their social mannerisms and by purchasing titles of nobility. See Asa Briggs, *Victorian People* (New York: Harper and Row, 1963), pp. 10–12.

[39] Atiyah, *op. cit.*, p. 234. Atiyah sees government action during the nineteenth century as a reaction to middle class complaints about specific problems, but it is clear that conservative politicians were important in achieving the necessary changes in government policy. See John Dewey, *Liberalism and Social Action* (New York: Capricorn Books, 1963 [First published in 1935]), pp. 20–22; E. L. Woodward, *The Age of Reform, 1815–1870.* Vol. XIII of *The Oxford History of England* (Oxford: Clarendon Press, 1938), pp. 142–147, 430.

that were unattached to the theoretical systems, scientifically based or otherwise, justifying unrestrained capitalism. They were unimpressed by the demands of "laws" based on either evolution or classical economic doctrine. They saw moral justice, in addition of course to their own economic self-interest, as a more important criterion for government policy.[40] The English landed interests of the nineteenth century had inherited the belief that the ownership of property entailed obligations and duties to the community, and they regarded the individualistic justifications claimed for capitalistic enterprise as attempts by those owning new forms of property to escape their responsibility for the welfare of the less fortunate in society.[41]

The South appears to be the one area in the United States where the factors conducive to a viable conservative movement existed. And, in fact, previous to the Civil War this area did produce several attacks on the abuses of industrialism.[42] But the war and continuing concern with the Negro question really eliminated this area as a source of thought that was persuasive on a national scope.[43] Even the chances for national political power in the presidential elections of 1876 and 1896 were passed by in return for assurance of continued white dominance in the South.[44]

This brief comparison of the English and American experiences in the nineteenth century suggests one reason why Americans turned to various forms of scientific method to undergird their value assumptions in social analysis and criticism. In England, the conservatives provided a distinct, politically powerful form of social criticism that owed little to scientific social doctrine. But in this country, the lack of a viable political conservative movement left almost unchallenged the appeal to science as a justification for laissez fairism. When serious challenges to laissez faire attitudes did occur, the validity of the methods and conclusions of the physical sciences for social analysis was so widely accepted that

---

[40] Woodward, op. cit., pp. 50, 430; Crane Brinton, English Political Thought in the Nineteenth Century (Cambridge, MA.: Harvard University Press, 1949), p. 143.

[41] Brinton, loc. cit.

[42] See George Fitzhugh, "Sociology for the South" and William J. Grayson, "The Hireling and the Slave" in Eric L. McKitrick (ed.), Slavery Defended (Englewood Cliffs, N.J.: Prentice-Hall, 1963), pp. 34–50, 57–68; George Fitzhugh, Cannibals All! or Slaves Without Masters (Cambridge, MA.: Harvard University Press, 1960 [First published in 1856]).

[43] Merle Curti, The Growth of American Thought (Second edition; New York: Harper and Brothers, 1951), p. 447; Clement Eaton, The Freedom-of-Thought Struggle in the Old South (Revised and enlarged edition; New York: Harper and Row, 1964), pp. 210–214, 344–352; W. F. Cash, The Mind of the South (New York: Alfred A. Knopf, 1941), pp. 129, 134.

[44] On the election of 1896, see E. E. Schattschneider, The Semi-Sovereign People (New York: Holt, Rinehart and Winston, 1960), pp. 79–80; Cash, op. cit., pp. 168–170.

effective counter-attacks had to claim to be more scientific than their opponents. In this process, the role of government as an authoritative implementer of social values received little serious consideration. Government became, instead, merely a tool of those social interests striving for protection or dominance on specific issues.

Reinforcing the attraction of scientific arguments was the influence of the German educational process on several generations of American thinkers after 1850. Many of the large number of American students who attended German universities after this date were provided with the intellectual tools for thorough social analysis.[45] William Graham Sumner, for one, attested to the rigor of the German approach to social analysis.

> ...They...taught me rigorous and pitiless methods of investigation and deduction. Their analysis was their strong point.... [T]heir method of study was nobly scientific, and was worthy to rank, both for its results and its discipline, with the best of the natural science methods....[46]

As aids in their research, the Germans utilized extensively the seminar, monograph, learned periodical, and specialized library[47]—tools that were, at that time, sadly lacking in American institutions of higher learning.[48] When American students returned home, they disseminated the techniques of German research.[49] With the establishment of Johns Hopkins in 1876, entire schools of higher education adopted the German approach.[50]

Heavily under the influence of Hegel, German scholars generally placed social institutions in a historical and evolutionary context that encouraged continual evaluation of the usefulness of social institutions over time.[51] In this respect, the German approach meshed easily with the Darwinian influence that impacted on America shortly after the Civil War. Where the German university orientation and the American experi-

---

[45] Curti, *op. cit.*, p. 582; Charles Franklin Thwing, *The American and German University* (New York: The Macmillan Company, 1928), pp. 42–45.

[46] William Graham Sumner, *Essays of William Graham Sumner.* Edited by Albert Galloway Keller and Maurice R. Davie (New Haven: Yale University Press, 1934), vol. 1, p. 6.

[47] Curti, *op. cit.*, p. 582; Thwing, *op. cit.*, pp. 114–122, 130.

[48] Richard Hofstadter, "The Revolution in Higher Education" in Arthur M. Schlesinger, Jr. and Morton White (eds.), *Paths of American Thought* (Boston: Houghton Mifflin Company, 1963), pp. 269–273, 283–286.

[49] Thwing, *op. cit.*, pp. 43–45. John Dewey and Thorstein Veblen, for example, studied under faculty educated in Germany. See Morton G. White, *Social Thought in America* (Boston: Beacon Press, 1957), p. 159.

[50] Thwing, *op. cit.*, p. 53, n. 2 states that of the original Johns Hopkins faculty, few had not studied in Germany and thirteen had received doctorates there. See also Hofstadter, "The Revolution," p. 274.

[51] Eric F. Goldman, *Rendezvous with Destiny* (Revised edition; New York: Alfred A. Knopf, 1956), p. 80.

ence parted company was the emphasis given to the role of the state. Again reflecting Hegelian influences, German thinkers did not shy away from considering the state in a serious philosophical fashion. Nor did German politicians shrink from invoking state power for the implementation of value-laden goals. Obviously, such considerations were not part of the ideological make-up of the social Darwinistic followers of Spencer and, as events in America would have it, the reform Darwinists were so repelled by the rigidities of the Spencerians that they consciously refused to proffer substantive values, although they were willing to support a much greater degree of state action. They were, however, unwilling to provide a coherent philosophical rationale for such action.

Laissez Faire Becomes Public Policy

The proponents of limited government and economic individualism had widespread public support during much of the latter nineteenth and early twentieth centuries in the United States; and their views soon became part of the supreme law of the land as enunciated by the nation's highest court. The laissez faire position gained additional credence from the tremendous economic and technological advances that occurred during this period. As a result, many Americans became convinced that governmental power was not necessary for domestic prosperity; and, thus, they saw no need to formulate an articulate theoretical basis for government as a democratically responsive force for social direction.

William Graham Sumner and Minimal Government

The foremost academic spokesman for laissez faire ideas in latter nineteenth-century America was, without a doubt, William Graham Sumner. An instructor at Yale University from 1868 until the early twentieth century, Sumner spent the better part of the period from 1870 through the early 1890s popularizing the doctrine of limited government and individual freedom. He was more than a devotee of the ideas of Spencer, however. His thought represents a fairly comprehensive amalgam of the currents comprising the intellectual revolution of the time. Adherence to the ideas of individualism and laissez faire originated from his early acquaintance with the thought of the classical economists.[1] Much of his methodology seems to have been derived from his educational years spent abroad in Germany. His acceptance of Spencer's ideas and their Darwinian parallels originally stemmed not from the *Social Statics* but from the later *The Study of Sociology*.[2] Richard Hofstadter's statement

---

[1] Hofstadter, *Social Darwinism*, p. 52.
[2] *Ibid.*, p. 55.

that Sumner "brought together three great traditions of western capitalist culture: the Protestant ethic, the doctrines of classical economics, and Darwinian natural selection. . . ."[3] succinctly summarizes his importance to the American liberal tradition. Ironically, it was just this conjunction of ideological factors that ultimately was to undermine the claims of both the classical economists and the Spencerian individualists.

The tradition of the Puritan ethic strongly colored Sumner's liberalism. There was, in Sumner, little of the optimism about individual moral growth or social progress that pervaded Spencer's *Social Statics*. In further contrast to Spencer, Sumner's primary focus was capitalistic economic development. The keystone of his laissez faire system was material aggrandizement in the form of capital. Capital formation was the force of progress and, for their efforts in this direction, successful capitalists deserved recognition as the most meritorious in society.[4] The self-discipline necessary for capital formation was one of the highest virtues and characterized the worth of the "forgotten man," who worked hard, paid his bills, and provided for his family, as well as that of the more successful entrepreneur.[5] Where Sumner and Spencer were in close agreement was in their positions regarding the need to restrict state action. Sumner believed that "do-gooders" must be prevented from using the state to implement their "humanitarian" projects.[6] Competitive evolution must be allowed to operate unhindered.

> Let it be understood that we cannot go outside of this alternative; liberty, inequality, survival of the fittest; not-liberty, equality, survival of the unfittest. The former carries society forward and favors all its best members; the latter carries society downwards and favors all its worst members.[7]

The struggle for existence and advancement is hard. The most that one can expect is an equal chance.[8] The results from this equal beginning will, of course, be unequal, but one can only do one's best.

> . . . If any man is not in the first rank who might get there, let him put forth new energy and take his place. If any man is not in the front rank, although he has done his best, how can he be advanced at all? Certainly in no way save pushing down any one else who is forced to contribute to his advancement.[9]

As Sumner put the point in another context, the individual must be prepared to "root, hog, or die."[10]

---

[3] *Ibid.*, p. 51.
[4] William Graham Sumner, *What Social Classes Owe to Each Other* (Caldwell, ID.: Caxton Printers, 1974 [First published in 1883]), pp. 47–48, 54–55, 68.
[5] *Ibid.*, pp. 110, 114–115, 125–126.
[6] *Ibid.*, pp. 13–22.
[7] Quoted in Hofstadter, *Social Darwinism*, p. 51.
[8] Sumner, *op. cit.*, pp. 141–142.
[9] *Ibid.*, p. 62.
[10] Quoted in Hofstadter, *Social Darwinism*, p. 54.

Sumner's view of government was similarly simple. "At bottom there are two chief things with which government has to deal. They are, the property of men and the honor of women...."[11] It was definitely not the function of government to make everyone happy.[12] Ameliorative schemes by those aiming to save mankind existed in abundance, but efforts by government to implement them resulted only in waste and in punishing those forgotten men who through hard work provided for themselves.[13] Sumner abruptly dismissed German efforts to provide philosophical bases for the state[14] and criticized the tendency of the English liberals to increase government functions once they attained power.[15] Abstractly, Sumner asserted, the state is simply "all-of-us." "In practice ... it is only a little group of men chosen in a very haphazard way by the majority of us to perform certain services for all of us...."[16] Because, for Sumner, it was the duty of every person to take care of himself or herself, the state owed the citizenry nothing beyond "peace, order, and the guarantees of rights."[17]

Although he had little faith in the elected representatives in American government, Sumner placed considerable confidence in the judiciary.[18] As will be demonstrated later, this confidence was certainly not misplaced, for during Sumner's lifetime the Federal and state courts moved toward increasing the viability of contract as a form of economic relationship free from government intervention. From Sumner's point of view, the higher status accorded to contracts in society was the mark of an advanced civilization,[19] and, in addition to arguing for the rights of entrepreneurs, he was strongly supportive of laborers' rights of private association to protect their interests.[20] The courts during this period, however, were not to be as favorable to organizational rights of labor as Sumner would have been. Generally they stood instead as bulwarks of protection for the constitutional rights of property.

The ideas of social Darwinism, or conservative Darwinism as some would have it, permeated American intellectual activity, encompassing related ideas in "economics, religion, morals, psychology, biology, history, law, and philosophy."[21] The interrelationship of these concepts consti-

---

[11] Sumner, *op. cit.*, p. 89.
[12] *Ibid.*, pp. 30–31.
[13] *Ibid.*, pp. 100–102, 129. Sumner noted: "We must not overlook the fact that the Forgotten Man is not infrequently a woman...." *Ibid.*, p. 126.
[14] *Ibid.*, pp. 8–9.
[15] *Ibid.*, p. 85.
[16] *Ibid.*, p. 9.
[17] *Ibid.*, p. 11.
[18] *Ibid.*, pp. 28–29, 94–96.
[19] *Ibid.*, pp. 23–24.
[20] For Sumner's views on labor associations, see *ibid.*, pp. 78–87, 96.
[21] Goldman, *op. cit.*, p. 67.

tuted what Eric Goldman has termed "a steel chain of ideas" that precluded government from a positive role in society.[22] These ideas were, of course, buttressed by those of the classical economists, who traced their roots to the Manchester school of economics and ultimately to Adam Smith. The classical economists were not Darwinian and would have preferred not to have been connected to evolutionary claims.[23] Their system was based on the belief in economic laws that were unchangeable in their operation, but that, like the position of the Spencerian evolutionists, emphasized limited government and individual enterprise. Despite the intellectual power of these schools of thought, they were not sufficient in persuasiveness to prevent attempts by the disadvantaged to invoke governmental aid. The efforts at increased governmental action tended to be piecemeal in approach and were really searching for some kind of ideological framework in which to operate, as evidenced by the tremendous popularity that Henry George's single tax scheme engendered. These efforts tended to receive harsh treatment in the courts.

Judicial Policy and Ideological Individualism
The ideas justifying laissez fairism found strong support in the American courts. Legislatures and executives might find it politic to respond to calls for governmental action, but the courts stood firm for decades against such efforts. In the latter nineteenth century, at the national level, such comprehensive efforts as a national income tax, the Interstate Commerce Commission, and the Sherman Anti-trust Act were either killed or substantially weakened by the Supreme Court.[24] In fact, the Supreme Court exercised a strong check on governmental action until 1937,[25] when FDR finally forced a reorientation in its approach to activist government.

The status of American courts stems from a number of factors, but there is little doubt that much of their prestige originally arose from their protection of property rights. This emphasis was clearly one of the axioms of Chief Justice John Marshall's constitutional theory, if not the primary one.[26] With the emergence of comprehensive philosophical rationales for laissez faire after the Civil War, the Supreme Court moved

---

[22] *Ibid.*, pp. 66–72.
[23] See *ibid.*, pp. 88–89; Fine, *op. cit.*, p. 202; Hofstadter, *Social Darwinism*, pp. 143–145.
[24] The relevant cases are: *Pollock* v. *Farmers' Loan and Trust Co.* 158 US 601 (1895)—income tax; *I.C.C.* v. *Cincinnati, New Orleans, and Texas Pacific Railway Co.* 167 US 479 (1897) and *I.C.C.* v. *Alabama Midland Ry. Co.* 168 US 144 (1897)—Interstate Commerce Commission; *U.S.* v. *E.C. Knight Co.* 156 US 1 (1895)—Sherman Anti-Trust Act.
[25] See Robert H. Jackson, *The Struggle for Judicial Supremacy* (New York: Vintage, [n.d.] First published in 1941).
[26] See Beryl Harold Levy, *Our Constitution* (Port Washington, N.Y.: Kennikat Press, 1965 [First published in 1941]), pp. 7–11.

easily to restricting and discouraging legislation that would limit property rights.

In their decisions and in their ideological posturing, the American courts have played an influential and, at times, determinative role in the failure of American liberalism to develop coherent ideological support for governmental authority. The Supreme Court justices enhanced their image in the public eye by projecting a stance of neutrality in their legal pronouncements. Drawing on an Anglo-American judicial tradition that dates at least to Justice Edward Coke's defense of the common law of England against the intervention of James I, American judges claimed that the study and application of the law required an artificial, specialized kind of reason that essentially removed the judge's personal biases from the decision process and relied solely on the law as discovered by their trained minds. Roscoe Pound, one of the moving forces for change in this legal attitude, was later to refer to this approach deprecatingly as "mechanical jurisprudence," or the "slot machine theory of law." Nonetheless, the image of neutrality projected by American judges protected them from public criticism at a time when, in historical retrospect, it can be seen that they were reading many laissez faire assumptions into constitutional doctrine. Thus, the most passive branch of American government gained in popular prestige at the same time that it inhibited efforts at more expansive application of governmental authority.

Despite their exclusion from the formulation and passage of legislation, American courts, nonetheless, make law in a very real sense. With the power of judicial review, they have the authority to overrule acts of legislatures and executives. The decisions of the Supreme Court are, barring amendment, accepted as the final interpretations of the Constitution and thus are the supreme law of the land in a way in which the acts of Congress can not be. Moreover, the decisions of U.S. courts make law in other, less spectacular, ways. Numerous legal commentators have pointed out that courts must decide cases where there is no statute law to guide them and must apply general laws to specific instances, often never contemplated by the authors of the statutes. In both of these instances, courts make the law in a tangible sense, and, under the Anglo-American common law system, would be exceptionally important policy-making bodies even without the power of judicial review. Thus, when the U.S. Supreme Court accepted the doctrines that asserted the general irrelevance of government for progress, these doctrines became an important influence on public policy as well as public opinion.

From the *Slaughterhouse Cases* decision,[27] which is often taken as the beginning of the modern era of constitutional interpretation, until the beginning of 1937 with the *West Coast Hotel* v. *Parrish* decision,[28] the U.S.

---

[27] 16 Wallace 36 (1873).
[28] 300 US 379 (1937).

Supreme Court, lower Federal courts, and state courts showed a decided sympathy to the rights of property and contract. This era of constitutional interpretation has been analyzed ably in many places,[29] but essentially it consisted of a gradual reinterpretation of constitutional clauses to incorporate laissez faire doctrine into the highest law of the land. During this period, the rights of corporate property were at a premium; the rights of the disadvantaged—the working class, blacks, children—tended to fall outside the sphere of constitutional protection. This development flowed not only from laissez faire economic doctrine, but also, as evidenced by some fairly specific statements by members of the Court, from social Darwinistic considerations as to the betterment of the race. The legal specifics were accomplished through restrictive interpretation of the extent of national delegated powers, such as those of taxation and commerce, and through limitation of state police power through the use of the due process clause of the Fourteenth Amendment. Blacks, in particular, suffered from restrictive interpretations of the equal protection clause of that amendment as well.

Although numerous justices during this period personally subscribed to the liberal individualism of laissez faire doctrine, three—Stephen J. Field, Rufus Peckham, and George Sutherland—are particularly noteworthy. Field saw the limitation of state activity move from his dissenting opinions to become the doctrine of the Court and the land. Peckham, probably the least able of the three, rendered several opinions that encapsulate the majority's thinking on the issue of state power versus individual rights. And Sutherland, an able justice by almost any standard, was a highly influential spokesman on the Court during the early twentieth century.

In the *Slaughterhouse Cases*, which constitutes the first extensive interpretation of the Fourteenth Amendment by the Supreme Court, Justice Miller, speaking for the majority, allowed Louisiana to regulate the trade of butchers through a statute granting a monopoly as to the location for abattoirs in the state. But Field simply could not countenance such interference with the rights of property. In addition to making logical mincemeat of Justice Miller's evisceration of the privileges and immunities clause, Field made a strong statement for constitutional protection of free enterprise under that clause.

> This equality of right, with exemption from all disparaging and partial enactments, in the lawful pursuits of life, throughout the whole country, is the

---

[29] Alfred H. Kelly and Winfred A. Harbison, *The American Constitution* (Fifth edition; New York: W. W. Norton, 1976), pp. 468–579, 645–711; Jackson, *op. cit.*; Edward S. Corwin, "The Supreme Court and the Fourteenth Amendment" and "The Passing of Dual Federalism" in Edward S. Corwin, *American Constitutional History.* Edited by Alpheus T. Mason and Gerald Garvey (New York: Harper and Row, 1964), pp. 67–98, 145–164.

distinguishing privilege of citizens of the United States. To them, everywhere, all pursuits, all professions, all avocations are open without other restrictions than such as are imposed equally upon all others of the same age, sex, and condition.... The fourteenth amendment, in my judgment, makes it essential to the validity of the legislation of every State that this equality of right should be respected.... And it is to me a matter of profound regret that its validity [that of the Louisiana statute] is recognized by a majority of this court, for by it the right of free labor, one of the most sacred and imprescriptible rights of man, is violated. [Here Field cited Adam Smith.]...[30]

In later cases, Field moved to arguing that the liberty in the due process clause of the Fourteenth Amendment protected economic endeavor. In his dissent in *Munn v. Illinois*,[31] he was particularly concerned that a legislative majority could overrule the rights of property owners. The majority of the Court upheld the right of the Illinois legislature to regulate the charges of grain warehouses in Chicago. Field demurred.

If this be sound law, if there be no protection, either in the principles upon which our republican government is founded, or in the prohibitions of the Constitution against such invasion of private rights, all property and all business in the State are held at the mercy of a majority of its legislature....[32]

By the term "liberty," as used in the provision [of the Fourteenth Amendment] something more is meant than mere freedom from physical restraint or the bounds of a prison. It means freedom to go where one may choose, and to act in such manner, not inconsistent with the equal rights of others, as his judgment may dictate for the promotion of his happiness; that is to pursue such callings and avocations as may be most suitable to develop his capacities, and give to them their highest enjoyment.

The same liberal construction which is required for the protection of life and liberty, in all particulars in which life and liberty are of any value, should be applied to the protection of private property....[33]

... The decision of the court in this case gives unrestricted license to legislative will.[34]

By the 1890s, Field saw the principles of his earlier dissents become the bases for majority opinions of the Court. In *Chicago, Milwaukee & St. Paul Railway Company v. Minnesota*,[35] the Court asserted that it had the power under the Fourteenth Amendment to determine the reasonableness of railroad rates set by a state legislature or its agent, and in *Smyth v. Ames*[36] it struck down state-established rates as violative of the Fourteenth Amendment. This latter decision opened a long series of decisions where the Court utilized the due process clause of the Fourteenth Amendment to limit state attempts to regulate business.

---

[30] *Slaughterhouse Cases*, at 109–110.
[31] 94 US 113 (1877).
[32] *Ibid.*, at 140.
[33] *Ibid.*, at 142.
[34] *Ibid.*, at 148.
[35] 134 US 418 (1890).
[36] 169 US 466 (1898).

Field, of course, did not limit himself to protecting business enterprise from state encroachments. He reacted intensely against national efforts in this direction also. In the relatively inconclusive first decision on the constitutionality of the national income tax statute, where the Court was evenly divided, four to four, Field added a few comments of his own for the record. He opposed the income tax and saw the issues raised by it as going

> ...down to the very foundation of the government. If the provisions of the Constitution can be set aside by an act of Congress, where is the course of usurpation to end? The present assault upon capital is but the beginning. It will be but the stepping-stone to others, larger and more sweeping, till our political contests will become a war of the poor against the rich; a war constantly growing in intensity and bitterness....[37]

Upon rehearing that same year, the Court struck down the income tax statute, thus protecting the earnings of the captains of industry for a few additional years.[38]

Much of the development of constitutional doctrine during the years that Field was on the Court can be interpreted as a reflection of economic beliefs interspersed with concerns about the relationship between national and state power. With regard to racial issues, however, more purely social Darwinistic considerations occasionally arose. Again, the net result of the Court's decisions in this area was a limitation on the power of government to deal with social issues of this sort in an ameliorative fashion. Field, himself, had demonstrated considerable sympathy for the Chinese minority in California in his earlier judicial decisions at the circuit court level but, in his later years on the U.S. Supreme Court, he failed to protect either Chinese or Negro rights from state infringements.[39]

The two major decisions in the latter nineteenth century that were to limit Negro rights for decades thereafter were the *Civil Rights Cases*[40] and *Plessy* v. *Ferguson*.[41] In both decisions, the Court weakened the equal protection clause of the Fourteenth Amendment as a source of Negro protection against state discrimination. In the *Civil Rights Cases*, attempts to utilize Federal law to punish racial discrimination by businessmen were voided. The Court ruled that the equal protection clause allowed the Federal government to punish only state-sponsored racial discrimination. This case, more than the *Plessy* decision, has social Darwinistic ramifications because here private businessmen claimed freedom from state impediment. At the conclusion of his opinion detail-

---

[37] *Pollock* v. *Farmers' Loan and Trust Company* 157 US 429 (1895), at 607.

[38] *Pollock* v. *Farmers' Loan and Trust Company* 158 US 601 (1895).

[39] Robert G. McCloskey, *American Conservatism in the Age of Enterprise* (New York: Harper and Row, 1964), pp. 109–126.

[40] 109 US 3 (1883).

[41] 163 US 537 (1896).

ing the legal bases for the Court's position, Justice Bradley could not refrain from offering a few nuggets of sociological wisdom.

> When a man has emerged from slavery, and by the aid of beneficent legislation has shaken off the inseparable concomitants of that state, there must be some stage in the progress of his elevation when he takes the rank of a mere citizen, and ceases to be the special favorite of the laws...[42]

Although the facts of the case are not as compatible with a laissez faire social position, because Louisiana had legislatively separated the races on railway cars, the opinion of Justice Brown in *Plessy v. Ferguson* was not without related social commentary.

> ...The argument [of Plessy] also assumes that social prejudices may be overcome by legislation, and that equal rights cannot be secured to the negro except by an enforced commingling of the two races. We cannot accept this proposition. If the two races are to meet on terms of social equality, it must be the result of natural affinities, a mutual appreciation of each other's merits and a voluntary consent of individuals. As was said by the court of appeals of New York in *People v. Gallagher* ... "...When the government, therefore, has secured to each of its citizens equal rights before the law and equal opportunities for improvement and progress, it has accomplished the end for which it is organized and performed all of the functions respecting social advantages with which it is endowed." Legislation is powerless to eradicate racial instincts or to abolish distinctions based upon physical differences, and the attempt to do so can only result in accentuating the difficulties of the present situation....[43]

The Plessy decision resulted in the infamous "separate-but-equal" doctrine, and it seems reasonably clear that the Court's general antipathy toward government action, here that of national intervention in the states, played an important role in its reaching its decision.

It might be further noted that neither of the foregoing decisions was rendered by a close vote. The *Civil Rights Cases* was an 8–1 decision, that of *Plessy v. Ferguson* 7–1 with Brewer not participating. Justice Harlan dissented in each case.

The tenure of Rufus Peckham overlapped with the last two years of Justice Field's service on the Court, although Field was often out of contact with reality in those last years. Peckham's devotion to individual liberties and restraint on government action was as intense as that of any justice on the Court before or since. In *Jacobson v. Massachusetts*,[44] Jacobson challenged the state's compulsory vaccination law, not on religious grounds, but on the basis that it infringed other rights under the Constitution. Harlan, speaking for the Court, disposed of Jacobson's plea on the basis of the state's police power to provide for the health of its citizens. Peckham and Brewer, Justice Field's nephew, dissented without comment. Given the instances where Peckham spoke out strongly for

---

[42] *Civil Rights Cases*, at 25.
[43] *Plessy v. Ferguson*, at 551.
[44] 197 US 11 (1905).

individual rights, one might suspect that Peckham saw Jacobson's right to risk the infection of small pox as more fundamental than the state's police power.

Of more importance in the development of American law was Peckham's success in reading the concept of liberty of contract into the Constitution, thus moving an important value of Sumner's thought into the realm of public policy. Peckham's opportunity came in the case of *Allgeyer* v. *Louisiana*[45] when Louisiana's statute forbidding contracts with out-of-state insurance companies was challenged. The law of the case is largely irrelevant for present purposes, but Peckham's new interpretation of the content of the word "liberty" in the Fourteenth Amendment spoke directly to the substance of laissez faire thought of the time.

> ... The liberty mentioned in that amendment [Fourteenth] means, not only the right of the citizen to be free from the mere physical restraint of his person, as by incarceration, but the term is deemed to embrace the right of the citizen to be free in the enjoyment of all his faculties; to be free to use them in all lawful ways; to live and work where he will; to earn his livelihood by any lawful calling; to pursue any livelihood or avocation, and for that purpose to enter into all contracts which may be proper, necessary, and essential to his carrying out to a successful conclusion the purposes above mentioned.[46]

In support of his interpretation, Peckham cited an earlier concurring opinion by Justice Bradley and a majority opinion by Justice Harlan that generally followed his individualistic economic orientation with regard to the Fourteenth Amendment.[47] Neither, however, appears to have used the term "contract" in its definition of liberty, and that addition was to be the important point of Peckham's approach.

The ideological and legal possibilities of the inclusion of liberty of contract under the protection of the Fourteenth Amendment surfaced most starkly in the now historic decision by Justice Peckham in *Lochner* v. *New York*.[48] This case revolved around the attempt of the New York legislature to limit the number of hours that bakers could work in a day and in a week, a subject which Spencer had used in *Social Statics* as an example of the lengths to which the paternalistic state might go.[49] Peckham responded to the New York effort in a style that would have endeared him to the original spokesman for social competition. He began by asserting that the right to make a contract for business purposes was a part of the protection provided under the Fourteenth Amendment and that this legislation interfered with contracts between employer and employees.[50] Much of his opinion was then devoted to showing that

---

[45] 165 US 578 (1897).
[46] *Ibid.*, at 589.
[47] *Ibid.*, at 589–590.
[48] 198 US 45 (1905).
[49] Spencer, *Social Statics*, p. 255.
[50] 198 US 45 (1905), at 53.

bakers were fully capable of entering into economic relationships on their own volition. "There is no contention that bakers as a class are not equal in intelligence and capacity to men in other trades or manual occupations, or that they are not able to assert their rights and care for themselves without the protecting arm of the State ... They are in no sense wards of the State...."[51] Later, in a bit of caustic understatement, he noted that "[v]ery likely physicians would not recommend the exercise of that or of any other trade as a remedy for ill health...."[52] At points, his pattern of argument *ad horrendum* follows very closely that of Spencer's earlier approach. Having listed examples of other trades that might also feel the weight of state intervention if the baker statute were upheld, he concluded that "[n]o trade, no occupation, no mode of earning one's living, could escape this all-pervading power...."[53] Peckham, it appears, was convinced that the use of state police power to protect the public safety and welfare was mere subterfuge for interests intent on undermining individual freedom. "It is impossible for us to shut our eyes to the fact that many of the laws of this character, while passed under what is claimed to be the police power for the purpose of protecting the public health or welfare, are, in reality, passed from other motives...."[54]

The decision in Lochner was the result of a close 5–4 vote. Justice Harlan, in dissent, took the majority to task on fairly straightforward legal issues, although he, too, was willing to grant the existence of a liberty of contract protection in the Constitution. Also dissenting, Justice Holmes spoke directly to the ideological aspects of Peckham's majority opinion.

> This case is decided upon an economic theory which a large part of the country does not entertain.... The liberty of the citizen to do as he likes so long as he does not interfere with the liberty of others to do the same, which has been a shibboleth for some well-known writers, is interfered with ... by every state or municipal institution which takes his money for purposes thought desirable, whether he likes it or not. The 14th Amendment does not enact Mr. Herbert Spencer's Social Statics....[55]

It would be easy to misread the focus of Holmes's dissent as an attack on social Darwinism. In fact, Holmes himself supported the postulates of social and economic survival of the fittest.[56] His point was that judges, as judges, had no right to interject their particular ideological preferences into interpretation of the Constitution. Unfortunately for Holmes's position and despite his rather plaintive assertion concerning "Mr. Herbert

---

[51] *Ibid.*, at 57.

[52] *Ibid.*, at 59.

[53] *Ibid.*; cf. Spencer, *Social Statics*, pp. 255–256.

[54] *Lochner v. New York*, at 64.

[55] *Ibid.*, at 75.

[56] See Samuel J. Konefsky, *The Legacy of Holmes and Brandeis* (New York: Collier Books, 1961), pp. 32–34.

Spencer," that was essentially what had happened by the time of the Lochner case. Although one would not expect the logical rigor or fine detail of the positions of Spencer and Sumner to be translated into public policy, still the general ideological orientation of these thinkers had strong support among the justices of the Supreme Court and thus became part of the supreme law of the land.

Constitutional limits on governmental authority did not prevent all efforts at social and economic reform. Legislation to strengthen the Interstate Commerce Commission was enacted in 1906, and legislation dealing with perceived social ills not related to economic enterprise generally received support from the Court. Even statutes limiting hours, first for women and then for men, were finally accepted by the Court.[57] Nonetheless, the Court's use of the ideology of laissez faire remained a powerful damper on the exercise of governmental power.

Representative of the Court in many ways during the 1920s and '30s was Justice George Sutherland. Alpheus Mason and Richard Leach note that, of the 320 opinions that he rendered while on the Court, 295 were with or for the majority and conclude that "[f]or sixteen years . . . his creed was in effect the supreme law of the land."[58] Sutherland was not without sympathy for the plight of the disadvantaged,[59] but in his mind the virtues of individual endeavor and the permanence of constitutional limits on government activity overrode the desirability of ameliorative government intervention. When the Court, in 1934, upheld Minnesota legislation designed to ease the burden of mortgages at that time of economic depression, Justice Sutherland dissented.

> . . . The vital lesson that expenditure beyond income begets poverty, that public or private extravagance, financed by promises to pay, either must end in complete or partial repudiation or the promises be fulfilled by self-denial and painful effort, though constantly taught by bitter experience, seems never to be learned; and the attempt by legislative devices to shift the misfortune of the debtor to the shoulders of the creditor without coming into conflict with the contract impairment clause has been persistent and oft-repeated.[60]

The mortgagors of Minnesota, in their attempts to obtain succor through legislative action, were in essence undermining the American constitutional system. "If the provisions of the Constitution be not upheld when they pinch as well as when they comfort, they may as well be abandoned. . . ."[61] Sutherland reasserted his status quo position in a later

---

[57] *Muller* v. *Oregon* 208 US 412 (1908); *Bunting* v. *Oregon* 243 US 426 (1917).

[58] Alpheus Thomas Mason and Richard H. Leach, *In Quest of Freedom* (Englewood Cliffs, N.J.: Prentice-Hall, 1959), p. 451.

[59] *Ibid.*, p. 448.

[60] *Home Building and Loan Association* v. *Blaisdell* 290 US 398 (1934), at 471–472.

[61] *Ibid.*, at 483.

dissenting opinion when he declared that "the meaning of the Constitution does not change with the ebb and flow of economic events. . . ."[62]

Sutherland's opinion for the majority in *Adkins* v. *Children's Hospital*[63] reflected his concern about the continued challenges to liberty of contract. The case involved Court review of the congressional statute establishing an administrative board to determine the minimum wage level for women employed in the District of Columbia. Sutherland's growing antipathy toward administrative agencies that exercised quasi-legislative duties[64] surfaced in the considerable space that he devoted to disparaging the legislative guidelines that were to provide the basis for action by the board. The main thrust of his opinion, however, rested on his conclusion that the minimum wage law contravened the role of contract in society by forcing the employer to pay a specific wage regardless of employee productivity.

> . . .To the extent that the sum fixed exceeds the fair value of the services rendered, it amounts to a compulsory exaction from the employer for the support of a partially indigent person, for whose condition there rests upon him no peculiar responsibility, and therefore, in effect, arbitrarily shifts to his shoulders a burden which, if it belongs to anybody, belongs to society as a whole.[65]

The statute was "so clearly the product of a naked, arbitrary exercise of power that it cannot be allowed to stand under the Constitution of the United States."[66]

Until 1937, when the challenge of FDR to enlarge the Court forced the justices to retreat from the limiting of government attempts to legislate in the economic sphere, the laissez faire justices on the Court continued to apply their principles as the law of the land. In their actions and ideology, they represented a belief system that was often dominant in America from about 1870 until at least 1932. On its face, this set of beliefs dealt with the question of governmental power clearly and directly; governmental activity should be held to a minimum because individuals could improve themselves and society most effectively by being allowed or forced to rely on their own capabilities. Closer inspection of this position within its social context suggests, however, that this reading of Court enforced laissez faire is superficial and detrimental to an accurate understanding of the forces of social control at work.

One problem with this interpretation of what was happening in society was that it assumed—this is especially true of Spencer—that authoritative direction of society was not really necessary and, if any-

---

[62] *West Coast Hotel* v. *Parrish* 300 US 379 (1937), at 402.

[63] 261 US 525 (1923).

[64] Mason and Leach, *op. cit.*, pp. 447–448.

[65] *Adkins* v. *Children's Hospital*, at 557–558.

[66] *Ibid.*, at 559.

thing, would be harmful. It failed to recognize that society was in fact receiving authoritative direction in a meaningful fashion from the nation's judges. A narrow view of governmental activity during this period could easily conclude that governmental powers were being limited and weakened when, in reality, the judicial branch of government was establishing a position of authority and public approbation that has rarely, during peacetime, been equaled by a democratic governmental institution. Bereft of the means for enforcing their decisions, the courts of America, nonetheless, demonstrated that constitutionally weak agencies could establish sufficient authority in the public mind to allow them to play an active, determinative role in the formulation of policy.

Most important, the policy role of the Supreme Court extended far beyond its specific decisions, for, in refusing to allow extensive governmental intervention in society, it was deferring to existing forms of social control. The heyday of laissez faire ideology in America was a period of tremendous economic and scientific growth, but, from the perspective of the latter twentieth century, it was still in many ways a simple time—a time when simple ideas about man and his place were still functional bases for everyday living for most people. What is now more obvious is that behind these essentially unquestioned beliefs lay techniques of behavioral and social control that drew, in many ways, on Bentham's early suggestions and played an important role in the maintenance of social stability. Thus, the Supreme Court, during this period, played a definitive role in social control by preventing political interference with the social arrangements that operationalized non-governmental forms of social direction.

Forces of Social Control in an Era of Limited Government
In a work focusing on the development of liberal orientations toward authority, an extended treatment of social history is neither necessary nor feasible. It is important at this point, nevertheless, to look briefly at some of the forms of social control at work during the period under discussion. These forces of social control worked fairly effectively at this time and thus gave credence to an ideology of limited government. When, however, they lost their effectiveness, American society saddled with ideological laissez faire artifacts of an earlier era remained without a theoretical framework for substituting governmental direction and control in their place.

Language paradigms appear to have played a particularly important role in contributing toward stability during this period. The language of the time embodied the assumptions of laissez faire individualism and, at the same time, elevated the status of those institutions and classes that implemented these assumptions.

Rhetorical embellishment significantly enhanced the status of the judiciary at this time. Eric Goldman asserts that, after the Civil War, "the Constitution reached a position of near-sacredness...."[67] The judiciary strengthened its position by assuming the stance of neutrally applying the rules contained in this all-seeing document. As late as 1936, Justice Owen Roberts, in a majority opinion, could say:

> ... It is sometimes said that the court assumes a power to overrule or control the action of the people's representatives. This is a misconception.... [The court] ... has only one duty,—to lay the article of the Constitution which is invoked beside the statute which is challenged and to decide whether the latter squares with the former.... This court neither approves nor condemns any legislative policy. Its delicate and difficult office is to ascertain and declare whether the legislation is in accordance with, or in contravention of, the provisions of the Constitution; and, having done that, its duty ends....[68]

While this posture toward the role of adjudicating aided in freeing economic enterprise, the Supreme Court, it must be remembered, showed no serious inclination to advance other forms of individual liberty during this period. It was 1925 before any of the First Amendment protections were applied by the Court against the states and, of course, the explosion in rights detonated by the Warren Court was still far in the future.

The conditions of economic opportunity in America, combined with the rhetoric of individual endeavor and reward, must have gone far toward mitigating unrest on the part of the masses. The popularity of Horatio Alger's rags-to-riches stories is well known even today, and Russell Conwell's "Acres of Diamonds" speech was given by him thousands of times throughout the country. It was, he proclaimed to his audiences, God's wish that they become rich.[69] These ideas were effective because people believed in them, and people believed in them because they saw tangible manifestations of them. As one commentator has noted, socialism in America was drowned in "reefs" of roast beef and apple pie.[70]

On the other hand, language played a far more oppressive role where the seriously disadvantaged blacks were concerned. Here America was crude and vicious, even in the more liberated northern areas. Textbooks and much popular literature portrayed blacks in a disparaging manner, and references to them in the vernacular operated to instill a sense of inferiority or servitude. It was with good reason that an important part of

---

[67] Goldman, *op. cit.*, p. 68.

[68] *U.S.* v. *Butler* 297 US 1 (1936), at 62.

[69] "I say, then, you ought to have money. If you can honestly attain unto riches in Philadelphia, it is your Christian and godly duty to do so...." Russell H. Conwell, *Acres of Diamonds*. Together with *His Life and Achievements* by Robert Schackleton (New York: Harper and Row, 1915), p. 20.

[70] Daniel Bell, *The End of Ideology* (New, revised edition; New York: Collier Books, 1962), p. 277 quoting Werner Sombart.

the Black Movement of the 1960s focused on the use of language with regard to black Americans.[71]

Michel Foucault has argued that the capitalistic bourgeois societies emphasizing the primacy of contract exercised more control over individuals than did the pre-French Revolutionary authoritarian regimes.[72] Foucault is concerned in *Discipline and Punish* with the growth of liberalism during the eighteenth and early nineteenth centuries, but his generalizations provide insight into the era of laissez faire ideology in America. Across the spectrum of capitalist society, he claims, institutions developed a "carceral continuum" that utilized the totalitarian principles of Bentham's panopticon scheme.[73] Important sectors of society were characterized by disciplines that created a kind of "political anatomy" through which life in institutions was monitored in detail.[74] Thus arose a diffusion of power acting in effective fashion throughout society.[75] "The contract may have been regarded as the ideal foundation of law and political power; panopticism constituted the technique, universally widespread, of coercion. . . ."[76] The "scientific-disciplinary mechanisms" extended to the prisons, schools, hospitals, military, and workshops.[77] This control utilized the "inspecting gaze, a gaze which each individual under its weight will end by interiorising to the point that he is his own overseer, each individual thus exercising this surveillance over, and against, himself. . . ."[78] The social control thus engendered lowered substantially the possibility of rebellion.[79] With appropriate reservations with regard to less centralized institutions, such as those in education, and the lower status of the military, Foucault's analysis is useful for interpreting the American experience. Certainly, the efficiency management pioneered by Frederick W. Taylor at the end of the nineteenth

---

[71] See Malcolm X, *The Autobiography of Malcolm X*. With the assistance of Alex Haley (New York: Ballantine Books, 1965), pp. 162–163.

[72] "The bourgeoisie is perfectly well aware that a new constitution or legislature will not suffice to assure its hegemony; it realizes that it has to invent a new technology ensuring the irrigation by effects of power of the whole social body down to its smallest particles. And it was by such means that the bourgeoisie not only made a revolution but succeeded in establishing a social hegemony which it has never relinquished. . . ." Michel Foucault, *Power/Knowledge*. Edited by Colin Gordon (New York: Pantheon Books, 1980), p. 156. See also Michel Foucault, *Discipline and Punish*. Translated by Alan Sheridan (New York: Pantheon Books, 1977), pp. 82–85.

[73] Foucault, *Discipline and Punish*, pp. 297–298.

[74] *Ibid.*, pp. 138, 177.

[75] *Ibid.*, p. 216.

[76] *Ibid.*, pp. 222, 303.

[77] *Ibid.*, pp. 138, 183, 218, 305.

[78] Foucault, *Power/Knowledge*, p. 155.

[79] *Ibid.*; Foucault, *Discipline and Punish*, p. 216.

century provided but a more sophisticated form of the control of human behavior analyzed for an earlier period by Foucault.[80]

Finally, the more obvious power relations created by capitalism must receive at least passing notice. Throughout the nineteenth century, there were critics separated as far ideologically as the Marxists and apologists for southern slavery who called attention to the crass, inhumane side of industrialism. Under capitalism, the entrepreneur had no responsibility for his workers outside of the factory. Illness or injury left them to their own devices, as did downturns in the economic cycle. Consistent laissez faire thinkers such as Sumner could call for trade union activity, but the men of property did not hesitate to use private police forces, the legislatures, and the courts to discourage such activity. Further, while these captains of industry could see the wisdom in preventing government intervention on behalf of the disadvantaged, they saw no serious problems with government activity on behalf of the advantaged. Thus, under the guise of a limited-government ideology, these interests were able to obtain numerous benefits, including land grants, protective tariffs, and policies that discouraged laborers from becoming too well organized.

In many respects, America of this period can be compared with England of the eighteenth century; in both instances, men of property had tremendous power while they operated from an ideological position of limited government that relied heavily on the courts to protect their interests. Additionally, in both periods, the common people were influenced by a rhetoric emphasizing their freedoms, which again, in each case, had some basis in fact. The English commoners of the eighteenth century were among the freest people in the world. The American working classes of the next century did have more economic opportunity than they would have had anywhere else in the world. Finally, both situations encouraged lack of attention to the ideological bases for governmental authority that could act in an expansive and directive fashion when needed.

---

[80] On Taylorism, see Curti, *op. cit.*, p. 652 and the comments of Michelle Perrot in Foucault, *Power/Knowledge*, p. 162.

Liberalism and Social Reform

GOVERNMENT AS THE REFLECTION OF SOCIAL DIVERSITY

The laissez faire position constructed by the Social Darwinists and the classical economists effectively stifled reform for decades. One of the important reasons for the power of the ideology of limited government was the fact that its proponents possessed conceptual explanations encompassing most social activities. Social arrangements might be seen as oppressive by many, but those offended by existing conditions, such as Henry George or the followers of the social gospel school, were limited in their attacks simply because they lacked a conceptual approach of comparable extent and appeal. Thus, piecemeal attacks on specific evils could have some effect, but the system itself remained in place. Nonetheless, while industrialists and other institutional forms of control prospered under the doctrine of limited government as enforced by the courts, the forces for pervasive change were beginning to take shape. For large segments of the population, rapid industrialization had created harsh conditions that were being more widely deplored. These conditions were exacerbated by the closing of the frontier. Moreover, reformers were publicizing the rapid strides toward industrialization that Germany had made through state aid to industry as well as to the working class. But just as important, perhaps most important, a new form of philosophy was coming to the fore. This new way of looking at the world explained man's place in society from a radically different perspective and meshed exceptionally well with the conceptual needs of the reformers.

As matters developed, the Achilles heel of Spencer's approach was to be his use of Darwin, an authority whom he had invoked some time after he had reached his basic conclusions justifying limited government and largely unfettered individual competition. His pragmatist opponents circumvented the static, status quo quality of his position, and that of the classical economists, by utilizing Darwin's ideas to support a changing conception of truth as more scientific. In fact, in the substantive sense, the pragmatist position as commandeered by John Dewey would be transformed into thoroughgoing epistemological relativism. Defining truth as relative and tying this relativism into practical politics gave a tremendous boost to the immediate causes of reform and injected a heavy dose of relativism into all social activities. This effect was further reinforced by Dewey's nominalism and egalitarian assumptions. Under this new perspective, government was removed from its constitutional pedestal and fashioned into a tool for social interests. The reformers could make government completely dependent on social interests because they assumed the existence of a basic social harmony and, in fact, social cooperation, not competition, was an important part of their rhetoric. The danger of the reformers' position from a practical standpoint was that it burned the candle from both ends. While weakening governmental power, by depriving it of an independent reason for being, they were at the same time undermining, through their relativistic stance, the forces of social cohesion that they assumed and that made their view of government viable.

Philosophical Pragmatism

Even while Spencer's ideas were enjoying tremendous popularity in the United States, the ideas of Darwin were being interpreted in a different and more sophisticated fashion by a small group of American thinkers. Their version of the epistemological revolution caused by the theory of evolution was to provide the philosophical basis for a wide-ranging rationale for government reform that engulfed the Spencerian position as well as the ideas of the classical economists. It is important to note, however, that the progenitors of pragmatism among that small group of Cambridge intellectuals who met informally as the Metaphysical Club were philosophical reformers—not social reformers. They looked askance at Spencer's claims to be scientific, but, at the same time, individuals like William James and C. S. Peirce were not the devotees of process and of value relativism that later editions of pragmatism in a more socially relevant form were to give primacy. In fact, much of the stimulus for philosophical inquiry by these early pragmatists seems to have stemmed from their need to justify the existence of metaphysical absolutes in the face of the materialistic implications of Darwin's ideas.[1] This concern for substantive values suffered tremendously when the methodological and empirical focus of pragmatism was turned by later thinkers to the justification for social reform. The result was that government was seen as a tool for reform but was left without a firm normative foundation from which it could act.

---

[1] Kuklick, *op cit.*, pp. 61–62.

The composition of the Metaphysical Club, which met in the early 1870s in the Cambridge, Massachusetts area, reflected the alliance of science and philosophy that had been a recurring theme in Anglo-American liberal thought since Hobbes and was to continue as a major element in pragmatism. Kuklick lists James, Peirce, and Oliver Wendell Holmes, Jr., as the originators of the group.[2] Both James and Peirce were trained in the physical sciences, and, at this time, Peirce was employed by the U.S. Coast and Geodetic Survey. Chauncey Wright, who was perhaps the leading intellectual of the group, also was trained in science and was employed as a computer for the *Nautical Almanac*. The most important thinkers in the group could best be described as practicing scientists and amateur philosophers.[3] In fact, none of the members of the Metaphysical Club was a professional philosopher, as most of the rest of the group, like Holmes, were involved in either teaching or practicing law. The underlying concern among these early members of the Metaphysical Club appears to have been to construct a firm philosophical basis for human consciousness in a cosmic order that had been rearranged by Darwin's conclusions. From the perspective of most of these thinkers, this effort required a reconciliation of religious belief with science, for, in Kuklick's words, they believed that "a positive creed was necessary to human well-being."[4]

Considered one of the best minds in the Cambridge area, Chauncey Wright articulated forcefully the materialistic and open-ended implications of Darwin's ideas. An advocate of the importance of the experimental method and proficient in the fields of mathematics, physics, botany, and psychology,[5] Wright was highly critical of Spencer's claims to be scientific. Spencer's use of evolution was, in his view, scientifically useless because it discouraged continual inquiry and experiment through its postulation of teleological absolutes.[6] Contrary to Spencer's assertions, natural development among the flora and fauna was not a purposeful progression toward ultimate perfection. Organic beings evolved through chance mutations and adaptation to the environment. In his essay, "The Evolution of Self-Consciousness," written at the request of Darwin, Wright argued that even the human mind can be explained in its present state of development as the result of non-teleological adaptation.[7] Generally Wright's position was that proper scientific method and

---

[2] *Ibid.*, p. 47.
[3] *Ibid.*, pp. 46–48.
[4] *Ibid.*, p. 62.
[5] Edward C. Moore, *American Pragmatism* (New York: Columbia University Press, 1961), pp. 5–7.
[6] Edward H. Madden, *Chauncey Wright* (New York: Washington Square Press, 1964), pp. 59–62.
[7] Kuklick, *op. cit.*, pp. 74–76.

explanation must be consonant with the dynamics of the universe, and for him these were non-teleological and materialistically determined. The experimental approach to problems that moved from hypothesis to verification provided the flexibility and objectivity necessary for gaining understanding of nature and man's place therein.[8] In retrospect, Wright's position can be seen as the first salvo of the successful pragmatist attack on Spencerian concepts of science, and, in this respect, it provided the opening for undermining Spencer's objections to government efforts at social reform. At the same time, Wright's extension of materialistic explanations to the human consciousness posed a threat to metaphysical sources of free will that made his fellow Cambridge thinkers exceedingly uneasy.

Although he was not as immersed in Darwin's ideas as were Wright and James, Peirce could easily spot logical flaws in the position of the opposition, and he was sufficiently Darwinian in orientation to see the search for truth as inherently developmental, or evolutionary. As did Wright, Peirce believed that Spencer's assertion of absolutes in the laws of nature nullified his claim to be scientific. In his opinion, Spencer's ideas were "antiquated and ignorant."[9] Spencer, he charged, was not even a good student of evolution. "Spencer is not a philosophical evolutionist, but only a half-evolutionist—or, if you will, only a semi-Spencerian. Now philosophy requires thoroughgoing evolutionism or none."[10] In contrast to the superficialities of Spencer, Peirce developed, in detail and with considerable sophistication, a philosophical framework for a proper scientific approach to truth. Drawing on his studies of Kant, he coined the term "pragmatism" as a label for his approach, although James was the first to use the term in print.[11]

Peirce's exposition of scientific method emphasized continual experimentation and the importance of consequences that were verified by common agreement—both key elements in the approaches of James and John Dewey. Truth, in Peirce's system, was any position arrived at experimentally that found general agreement as to its veracity among those knowledgeable of it. "The opinion which is fated to be ultimately agreed to by all who investigate is what we mean by the truth, and the object represented in this opinion is the real. That is the way I would explain reality."[12] The "sensible effects" produced by an action consti-

---

[8] Madden, *op. cit.*, pp. 63–67.
[9] C. S. Peirce, "Concerning the Author" in Justus Buchler (ed.), *Philosophical Writings of Peirce* (New York: Dover, 1955), p. 2.
[10] C. S. Peirce, "The Architecture of Theories" in *ibid.*, p. 319.
[11] Kuklick, *op. cit.*, pp. 53–54. John Dewey, "The Development of American Pragmatism" in John J. McDermott (ed.), *The Philosophy of John Dewey* (New York: G. P. Putnam's Sons, 1973), vol. 1, pp. 41–42.
[12] C. S. Peirce, "How to Make Our Ideas Clear" in Buchler, *op. cit.*, p. 38.

tuted reality.[13] But, for a scientific explanation of reality to be constructed, the experimental approach of hypothesis and subsequent verification of the experimental results must be utilized. Furthermore, Peirce was clear that this process must remain open-ended, leaving the possibility for further investigations and different versions of reality.[14] Although Peirce confined himself fairly closely to philosophical questions, his approach carried egalitarian social implications once it was applied to social issues. If scientific truth was relative to the agreement reached on a point, then obviously truth in the social sphere could also be seen as dependent on the opinions of those affected.

Despite his focus on the empirical and the need for continual inquiry, Peirce would not have seen himself as an empiricist in the twentieth-century sense. He rejected religious skepticism and saw himself as working toward a reconciliation of science and religion. In his most famous essay, "How To Make Our Ideas Clear," Peirce suggested that behind his methodological concerns rested an assumption about the existence of an absolute truth.

> ...[R]eality is independent...of what you or I or any finite number of men think about it....Our perversity and that of others may indefinitely postpone the settlement of opinion; it might even conceivably cause an arbitrary proposition to be universally accepted as long as the human race should last. Yet even that would not change the nature of the belief, which alone could be the result of investigation carried sufficiently far....But the reality of that which is real does depend on the real fact that investigation is destined to lead, at last, if continued long enough, to a belief in it.[15]

The foregoing quotation conveys Peirce's faith that the valid application of mental processes will lead eventually to an articulated harmony between consciousness and the objectively real. Thus, as Kuklick has pointed out, Peirce saw pragmatism as more than a methodological tool, for he retained an attachment to conceptual absolutes that were metaphysically based and which he believed that proper method would establish as true.[16]

Peirce's attempts to place epistemological beliefs on a scientific footing had an immense influence on William James, who was searching for a functional definition of consciousness within the framework of evolutionary postulates. After Peirce left the Cambridge area to teach at Johns Hopkins, James remained an intellectual colleague and friend of his. This relationship continued until James's death, even though Peirce was forced to leave Johns Hopkins in some personal disgrace and was unable thereafter to obtain an academic appointment. As John Dewey put it,

---

[13] *Ibid.*, pp. 31, 36.
[14] *Ibid.*, pp. 28–29, 31, 35–36.
[15] *Ibid.*, p. 39.
[16] Kuklick, *op. cit.*, pp. 123, 126.

James brought the disembodied philosophical formulas of Peirce to the level of individual belief and action.[17] Although he was a graduate student at Johns Hopkins while Peirce was there, Dewey appears to have come to Peirce's ideas through the works of James, whose seminal two-volume *Principles of Psychology* (1890) was a particularly important influence on Dewey's acceptance of pragmatism.[18]

James was a thinker of considerable depth, perhaps greater depth than Dewey, and was unhesitatingly honest intellectually. He faced difficult epistemological and metaphysical questions directly and at times went for long periods when he acknowledged that he could find no solutions that met his criteria of acceptability. During the 1869-1870 period, he underwent a serious intellectual and emotional crisis engendered by his realization that Darwinian axioms applied to the mind meant that human consciousness was ultimately materially determined and that he and the rest of humanity were thus left without even a "wriggle" of free will. However, drawing on his reading of the work of the French neo-Kantian Charles Renouvier, James finally resolved his personal depression simply by asserting his belief in his free will and determining to act on the basis of that belief.[19]

James's determination to provide philosophical support for spontaneous change and creativity in the universe led to his rejection of Spencer's approach as a mechanistic, deterministic, even fatalistic interpretation of Darwin's ideas. Furthermore, the descriptive method that Spencer used was not science; it was but a beginning point for scientific investigation.[20] For James, as for Peirce, truth was found as the result of trial and error and was validated in the minds of concrete, experiencing individuals, not through statements asserting the existence of objective natural laws.

Not until the late 1890s did James announce himself as a philosophical pragmatist. Previous to this time, he wrote and spoke as a psychologist, and Kuklick argues that his inability to construct a satisfactory metaphysical alternative to Josiah Royce's absolute idealism inhibited him from taking a pragmatic position publicly. Intuitively, James was an idealist, but he found Royce's position too deadening to spontaneity for his taste.[21] The resolution to his intellectual impasse began with

---

[17] Dewey, *op. cit.*, pp. 44–45, 47.

[18] *Ibid.*, pp. 44–53.

[19] John Passmore, *A Hundred Years of Philosophy* (New York: Penguin, 1966), p. 101. The story of James's mental crisis is treated at length in Moore, *op. cit.*, pp. 110–116.

[20] William James, *The Will to Believe and Other Essays in Popular Philosophy* (New York: Dover Publications, 1956 [First published in 1897]), pp. 232–235; see also Kuklick, *op. cit.*, pp. 162, 174, 311.

[21] See Kuklick, *op. cit.*, pp. 179, 181, 264, 295.

his rejection of the British empiricist position that consciousness was something separate from the experienced material world. James asserted that it was instead part of a continuous, flowing experience of the world. An individual's consciousness encompassed everything in his experienced environment, and it was an act of mind itself that insisted on artificially compartmentalizing experience into subjective and objective elements.[22] The interaction of individual minds with their environments produced a variety of experiences leading to differing beliefs, a result that merely reflected the pluralistic nature of the universe.

Moving beyond Peirce's use of the idea of truth, James saw truth as determined by the satisfaction that an individual derived from a belief or action. For James, this view of truth was scientifically valid both in terms of his understanding of the scientific method as elucidated by Peirce and in terms of the conclusions that he had formed as a result of his psychological studies. Furthermore, truth in a Jamesian sense allowed for creativity and free will as individuals interacted with each other and the natural environment. Obviously, concepts of the truth would vary from individual to individual and over time as individuals discovered new experiences and thus judged the consequences of beliefs and actions differently. Because pragmatism posited truth as a changing standard, James could not logically argue that pragmatism itself embodied an absolute statement of truth. But he did assert that the pragmatic approach would remain valid in that, in the long run, everyone, no matter what his or her philosophical position, was guided by the criteria for truth used by pragmatism.[23]

James's integration of his idealist strivings into the pragmatic approach is illustrated in his arguments for the existence of God. Edward C. Moore has noted that the question of the existence of God pervaded James's philosophical endeavors.[24] This question also was an issue intimately tied into the early personal crisis that he experienced from his confrontation with the deterministic implications of evolutionary materialism. James acknowledged that the existence of God can not be proven scientifically, but, he asserted, neither can it be disproven. Nonetheless, the question of God's existence can not be avoided. Each individual *must* decide for himself, and, since this is the case, each individual is entitled to decide the question in a manner that is emotionally satisfying. Thus, each arrives at his or her truth with regard to the issue. But James argued that truth in this instance might also stem from the existence of a divine being, because belief in the existence of God can lead individuals to act in a fashion that enables them to live lives and achieve goals that

[22] Passmore, *op. cit.*, pp. 104–109.
[23] Kuklick, *op. cit.*, pp. 268–269, 325–334.
[24] This discussion draws heavily on Moore, *op. cit.*, pp. 116–134.

they otherwise might not. In this sense, belief in God engenders consequences that are satisfying in terms of inner peace and behavior in the
world. James added that evolutionary evidence, while it did not prove
God's existence, did tend to indicate the existence of God. It should be
noted, however, that James's view of God was more restrictive than the
traditional Judeo-Christian position.

> The line of least resistance, then, as it seems to me, both in theology and in
> philosophy, is to accept, along with the superhuman consciousness, the no-
> tion that it is not all-embracing, the notion, in other words, that there is a God,
> but that he is finite, either in power or in knowledge, or in both at once.[25]

As Moore has suggested, James's conception of a limited God enhanced
the importance of religious belief and practice as means of improving
the world, a ramification in keeping with James's attachment to free will.

For James, ultimate questions were an important concern of philosophy, and his determination to find a philosophical justification for
belief in God demonstrated that he continued to see metaphysically
based values as essential in a philosophical environment that was becoming increasingly empirical.[26] Indeed, in an especially revealing statement, James illustrated that the early pragmatists were not afraid to
articulate and live by normative values. Kuklick quotes James as declaring:

> Here in this room, we all of us believe in molecules and the conservation of
> energy, in democracy and necessary progress, in Protestant Christianity and
> the duty of fighting for the doctrine of the immortal Monroe, all for no reasons
> worthy of the name.[27]

Such a statement by John Dewey would have seemed quite out of place;[28]
for James it was merely an assertion of the principles by which he and
his fellow patrician New Englanders lived. This kind of open acknowl-
edgement of the importance of substantive values removes James and
his colleagues from the ascetic, empirical orientation of much of contemporary philosophy. In the words of Merle Curti: "In insisting on the reality
of values and purposes, James seemed . . . to have more sympathy with
traditional and spiritual than modern, scientific ideas."[29] In its disavowal
of the importance of substantive metaphysical values, Dewey's instru-

---

[25] Quoted in *ibid.*, p. 133 from William James, *A Pluralistic Universe* (New York:
Longmans, Green, and Co., 1909), p. 311.

[26] In addition to Moore, *loc. cit.*, see Kuklick, *op. cit.*, p. 316.

[27] Kuklick, *op. cit.*, p. 172.

[28] See the discussion in Darnell Rucker, *The Chicago Pragmatists* (Minneapolis:
University of Minnesota Press, 1969), p. 107, n. where Herbert Schneider's
description of Dewey's irritation at the attention given to his proposed lecture
on religion is recounted. See also generally John Dewey, *A Common Faith*
(New Haven: Yale University Press, 1934).

[29] Merle Curti, *Human Nature in American Thought* (Madison: University of
Wisconsin Press, 1980), p. 205.

mentalist derivation of pragmatism would be considered more scientific than James's approach and it, of course, fit well with the social reform movement in its attention to social issues. On the other hand, the drift in national policy that has resulted from the social implementation of a pragmatist philosophy stripped of substantive values might be an indication that an exceptionally important aspect of pragmatism was left behind in the comfortable circumstances of upper class nineteenth-century New England.

John Dewey: Philosophy and Politics in a Relativistic World

In terms of his influence on political thought, Dewey's ideas can be summarized under three themes: the rejection of universals, the assumption of the equality of human rationality, and the redefinition of philosophy as process and as the handmaiden of social reform. Although later developments have raised serious questions about its sociological and philosophical depth, Dewey's thought had the merits of logical coherence within a new scientific view and of appeal to important social interests.

From Dewey's instrumentalist perspective, the search for epistemological absolutes or universally applicable metaphysical truths was not a legitimate philosophical activity. "Philosophy forswears inquiry after absolute origins and absolute finalities in order to explore specific values and the specific conditions that generate them."[30] Throughout Dewey's thought runs the contention that philosophy should provide the method for dealing with changing human needs. There were, he asserted, two major philosophical responses to Darwin: one led to revision of traditional philosophical assumptions, and the other, represented by Spencer and his American disciples, resulted in a "recrudescence of absolutistic philosophies."[31] Dewey rejected individualistic liberalism as a form of "intellectual atavism."[32] It was an irony of history that the ideology of classical liberalism that had been so important in stimulating democratic advances now used the rhetoric of individual freedom to obstruct reform efforts to increase that freedom.[33] Philosophical attempts to discover universal values were detrimental to society because they diverted attention from the real problems in society. But, Dewey vowed, "[n]o longer will views generated in view of special situations be frozen into absolute standards and masquerade as eternal truths."[34] Philosophy,

---

[30] John Dewey, *The Influence of Darwin on Philosophy and Other Essays in Contemporary Thought* (New York: Henry Holt and Company, 1910), p. 13.

[31] *Ibid.*, p. 18.

[32] *Ibid.*, p. 14.

[33] John Dewey, *The Public and Its Problems* (Chicago: Gateway Books, 1946 [First published 1927]), pp. 95, 102, 109.

[34] *Ibid.*, p. 203.

if it was to keep pace with contemporary science, must become a method of inquiry that utilized the consequences of ideas and actions as the criterion of truth.[35]

Dewey's version of pragmatism was an amalgam of a variety of experiences and intellectual influences. His orientation toward social reform appears to have stemmed from his personal involvement in reform efforts such as Jane Addams's Hull House and from the fact that the universities at which he taught were initiators of much of the change being wrought in higher education in America.[36] Intellectually, the first important influence on his thought came from the German idealist G. W. F. Hegel. Hegel had constructed a comprehensive statement of dialectical change in the world and had viewed society as an organic entity in which individuals found meaning and freedom through their attachment to the social whole, a position diametrically opposed to the classical liberal view. Hegel's philosophical position was, in many respects, the antithesis of that of the British empiricists and much closer to the views of T. H. Green, a British idealist of the second half of the nineteenth century whom Dewey also admired. Although he moved away from much of Hegel as his ideas matured, Dewey retined an appreciation for the German thinker's perspective on society.[37] Hegel's idealism gave way, for Dewey, to the more empirical definition of consciousness given by the Cambridge pragmatists, in particular William James. Drawing heavily on James, Dewey came to see philosophy as a method for utilizing human intelligence for the achievement of satisfactory conditions of living as judged by those affected by those conditions. Darwin's ideas, of course, were also important to Dewey as they had been for his American predecessors. In Dewey's case, however, the scientific validity that Darwin gave to the concept of evolutionary social change probably served to reinforce the historicist position that he had already found in Hegel. Darwin's explanation of change dispensed with metaphysical forces, was essentially non-teleological, and was grounded in the behavior of living organisms. Thus, the methodological implications of Darwin's ideas were more appealing to Dewey than Hegel's reliance on the dialectical unfolding of Reason in the phenomenal world.[38] Clearly, the scientific support that Darwin appeared to give to the idea of thorough-going social change

[35] *Ibid.*, p. 74.

[36] See Goldman, *op. cit.*, pp. 121–122. Richard Bernstein asserts that after the 1890s Dewey was "America's intellectual spokesman for practical social reform." Richard J. Bernstein, *John Dewey* (New York: Washington Square Press, 1966), p. 37.

[37] John Dewey, "From Absolutism to Experimentalism" in McDermott, *op. cit.*, pp. 6–8; Bernstein, *op. cit.*, p. 12.

[38] Dewey, *Influence of Darwin*, pp. 1, 7–9, 11.

provided Dewey with the basis for launching telling attacks against the proponents of laissez faire.

Dewey's argument that philosophy was a method for dealing with pervasive change in the universe effectively undermined Spencer's position and wreaked serious damage to that of the classical economists, who argued for laissez faire from premises based on unchanging economic principles. This attachment to what were essentially metaphysical absolutes rendered the classical economists vulnerable to the charge of being unscientific, and Dewey did not hesitate to exploit this opening.[39] The classical economists, he charged, had failed to recognize the historical relativity of their position, a position that social change had rendered out of date. In twentieth-century America, progress resulted from social cooperation, not individualistic competition, and government was an important means for aiding in achieving progress.

As one can readily imagine, Dewey's conception of government differed markedly from the positions taken by those early liberals, Hobbes and Locke. For Dewey, government was not distinguished by accoutrements of authority or legitimacy so much as it was defined by the range of the consequences of its actions. The *raison d'être* of government was the adjustment of social policy in response to the demands of social interests with regard to specific problems that they deemed important.[40] Government was the process of applying social intelligence to these problems, and, as an entity, it was simply another social institution differing from others primarily in the extent of the consequences that it had for the public.[41] Government operating from an instrumentalist perspective would approach problems in an experimental fashion and evaluate the solutions attempted in terms of the effects that they had for individuals. Dewey decried the "holiness" with which the Constitution, the Supreme Court, and the institution of private property had been endowed as a continuation of absolutist thinking.[42] To be an effective tool, government must be capable of intervening in society when and where it is needed. Government could not be appropriately scientific if it was limited by ideological barriers erected by outmoded philosophical thinking.

For all of his discussion about the utilization of scientifically based philosophical approaches in government, Dewey's view of the citizen

---

[39] See John Dewey, *Liberalism and Social Action* (New York: Capricorn Books, 1963 [1935]), pp. 32–34. The position taken by Dewey was reinforced by the thoroughly evolutionary position taken by Sumner in his last book, *Folkways*. See William Graham Sumner, *Folkways* (Revised edition; Boston: Ginn and Company, 1911), pp. 4, 16–19, 35–36.

[40] Dewey, *The Public*, p. x; Dewey, *Liberalism*, p. 79.

[41] Dewey, *The Public*, pp. x, 27, 54, 174; Dewey, *Liberalism*, pp. 50, 79.

[42] Dewey, *The Public*, p. 170.

who would participate in such government was derived from what can only be described as a tremendous leap of faith on his part. His vision of the democratic citizen was thoroughly optimistic and egalitarian, characteristics that seemed to be inherent in his philosophical position.

> ...Instrumentalism, however, assigns a positive function to thought, that of *re*constituting the present stage of things instead of merely knowing it. As a consequence, there cannot be intrinsic degrees, or a hierarchy of forms of judgment. Each type has its own end, and its validity is entirely determined by its efficacy in the pursuit of its end. A limited perceptual judgment, adapted to the situation which has given it birth, is as true in its place as is the most complete and significant philosophic or scientific judgment....[43]

Locke's elevation of the industrious and the rational to positions of political leadership appears to have no support in Dewey's system of philosophy or democracy. Dewey's position was that each person is the best judge of his interests. "The man who wears the shoe knows that it pinches and where it pinches...."[44]

Dewey completed his egalitarian approach to democracy by redefining the concept of intelligence in a manner that drew on James's view of mind as a flow of consciousness but that departed dramatically from James's individualism. Thinking of intelligence as an individual characteristic was an anachronistic approach that obstructed constructive social change, Dewey asserted. Properly conceived, intelligence is a web of social relationships allowing for the communication and sharing of knowledge among the members of society so that each shares in scientific and technological advances.[45] Such a definition obviously contributed support to Dewey's belief in the essential equality of policy judgments among the citizenry. Nevertheless, Dewey's effort at redefinition does not remove the questions raised by his levelling approach to society. Simply defining away individualized intelligence does not erase the fact that some individuals, even among those living in roughly equivalent environments, are significantly more capable and rational than others, a position that James took.[46] Nor does it eliminate the issue raised by the relative worth of standards of judgment among individuals of varying degrees of competence and taste. Certainly, it provides little long-range guidance or support for a government that, by Dewey's definition, serves merely to adjust the differences in judgment that arise among interests in society.

In his discussions of democratic government, Dewey appears to have been thinking in terms of a reconstituted citizen, one who could be

---

[43] Dewey, "Development of American Pragmatism," p. 55.
[44] Dewey, *The Public,* p. 207.
[45] *Ibid.*, pp. 211, 219; Dewey, *Liberalism,* pp. 42–47, 52, 69.
[46] See James's essays "Great Men and Their Environment" and "The Importance of Individuals" in James, *op. cit.*, pp. 216–262.

trusted to make sound judgments and to act unselfishly, for he had reservations about the citizens of his day. He noted that individuals acted "from crudely intelligized emotion and from habit" and were easily diverted by amusements, and he expected that vested interests in a position to "manipulate social relations for their own advantage" would oppose the experimental method in government.[47] Although at one time he labelled the use of force by government as "unregenerate," he later indicated that it might have to be employed against entrenched and powerful minority interests.[48] To offset these problems, Dewey argued for a form of social organization that would facilitate education of the public on the virtues of the pragmatic approach to thinking about the world and to implementing public policy.[49] Dewey was personally involved in educational reform in the schools throughout his adult life, but he recognized that effective education for constructive civic activity had to be broader than formal education. Society should be organized to enable the freest flow of communication and information and to encourage individuals to realize their abilities through group participation.[50] The great society must become the great community, he urged.[51] Dewey did not specifically make such an enlightened context a prerequisite for the organized social planning that he advocated, but it is clear that a citizenry rising to the potential that he envisioned for individuals would have greatly facilitated a social engineering approach to public policy.

Throughout his writings, Dewey was circumspect in avoiding the advocacy of substantive goals. At one point, he asserted that it was not part of his "task to outline in detail a program for renascent liberalism."[52] Nonetheless, his writings convey the impression that economic reform was, in his mind, a major priority for action, and in *Liberalism and Social Action* his emphasis on the need for socialized control of the forces of production came very close to being an overt argument for socialism.[53] Dewey was careful in his works to avoid setting limits on the range of government activity, preferring instead to see these subject to experimental change,[54] and, in this respect, socialism would have been compatible with his instrumentalist thought. The point to be made here is not that advocacy of socialism would have been un-American of Dewey but that the openness of his approach made it vulnerable to use, or exploitation, by a wide variety of ideologies. There is no question of Dewey's attach-

---

[47] Dewey, *The Public,* pp. 56, 139, 158, 169.
[48] *Ibid.,* p. 154; Dewey, *Liberalism,* p. 87.
[49] Dewey, *Liberalism,* p. 53.
[50] *Ibid.,* pp. 31, 54–55, 58.
[51] Dewey, *The Public,* p. 142.
[52] Dewey, *Liberalism,* p. 91.
[53] *Ibid.,* pp. 54, 88–91.
[54] Dewey, *The Public,* pp. 64–65.

ment to democracy as a process,[55] but his jettisoning of the philosophical worth of substantive moral values made democracy a highly relative term—a term that was to be extended to cover governmental systems that Dewey would unquestionably have found totally unacceptable. Even within America, by the 1960s and 1970s the economic laissez faire that Dewey criticized had, with the aid of his philosophical reticence, been replaced by a moral and social laissez faire of disquieting proportions. This development received further support from the symbolic interactionist perspective of George Herbert Mead, another member of the Chicago School of pragmatism and a close friend and colleague of Dewey at that school and earlier at Michigan. Mead's thought will receive greater treatment later, but it can be noted here that his perspective has been an important theoretical school in sociology and has served to increase value relativity in dealing with social issues.

Dewey's thought was a product of its historical moment, just as were the ideas of those whom he accused of absolutism. His attacks on traditional philosophy as historically conditioned and an obstacle to progressive thought made him sensitive to the possibility that he might be substituting his moral absolutes for those that he attacked. At the same time, he firmly believed that philosophy must direct reform in America, and, while Spencer essentially ignored the state, Dewey did not hesitate to invoke its aid. He was able to use philosophy to do "good things" and yet avoid the charge of touting substantive biases of his own by conceiving of philosophy as method, or process. With Darwin's ideas apparently sanctioning change in the social sphere as well as in the biological and with the work that Peirce had done in the philosophy of science, Dewey had a basis for claiming that his instrumentalist version of pragmatism incorporated the most recent scientific thinking. Thus the scientific method transmitted through instrumentalism became philosophical truth and process at one and the same time, and Dewey's exposition of philosophy as a tool for change enabled him to avoid being charged with the same errors that he attributed to his critics. This stance in fact made it difficult to attack him at all, for his philosophy, to put it mildly, was an elusive and moving target. Although such ambiguity had defensive virtues in the arena of intellectual combat, it posed serious difficulties when instrumentalism was accepted as a useful rationale for public policy. Concentration on the consequences of actions and beliefs enabled government to focus on specific problems, but the standards by which these problems were to be defined or resolved were no longer a

---

[55] Charles Morris asserts that for Dewey democracy was a "moral conception." See Charles Morris, *The Pragmatic Movement in American Philosophy* (New York: George Braziller, 1970), p. 159.

part of the philosophical framework within which American pluralist democracy functioned.

In some respects, Dewey's attacks on absolutist philosophies served as a useful antidote to modes of thinking that had rigidified beyond a socially useful stage. But his acceptance of the social applicability of the methodology of the physical sciences raises again the question of the relevance of these methods for social relationships and, at the same time, provides evidence of an absolutist side to Dewey's thought. Dewey was highly relativistic with regard to substantive values, arguing that these varied in validity according to the social context. He refused, however, to consider the possibility that methods for dealing with problems might also vary in validity depending on the context. In other words, it is conceivable that the methods of the physical sciences are simply not appropriate for a wide range of social issues. The physical sciences, for the most part, deal with the objective and non-thinking portion of the world, where norms and values are meaningless and irrelevant. Such socially constructed and recognized standards are nonetheless essential to human existence and, contrary to the hopes of Hobbes, there is no scientific approach that can deal with them as objectively as the physical scientist deals with his materials. Individual human beings can at times, of course, be treated as mere objects, an approach that Dewey would have abhorred, but even then the cultural biases of the experimenters are an inextricable part of the science being performed.

In the final analysis, Dewey's attempt to apply scientific method to social policy had the deterministic implications that James feared. Dewey advocated democratic processes with moralistic fervor, but it is clear that his support for democracy was heavily reinforced by his belief that it constituted the equivalent of scientific method, or truth, in society. This conception of truth rested ultimately on natural causes, for Dewey simply would not countenance the legitimacy of universally valid metaphysical values, even in religion. In light of Einstein's firm belief that God does not play dice with the world, one would be in respectable scientific company in questioning Dewey's rejection of the metaphysical. As the essence of a creed by which individuals must give meaning to their lives, Dewey's system is spartan and even depressing. If one operates within the scientific paradigm that Dewey used, there may not be a logical answer to the dilemma that his approach poses, a possibility that obviously worried James. But history seems to indicate that individuals require an attachment to something more ethereal than satisfactory consequences of a material sort, and this suggests that there may exist paradigms of meaning more appropriate for human society than Dewey's instrumentalism. In this respect, the search for philosophically viable metaphysical values by James and Peirce would seem to reflect a better understanding of the nature of the human condition than that demonstrated by Dewey.

Judicial Policy as Social Engineering

The discussions of the Metaphysical Club had ramifications for the reorientation of legal thought as well as general philosophy. Of the six comprising the intellectual core of the group, three were scientists and three were lawyers.[56] Of the three lawyers—Nicholas St. John Green, Joseph Bangs Warner, and Oliver Wendell Holmes, Jr.—Holmes was to carry important elements of the pragmatic view into his studies of the law and into his opinions as a justice of the U.S. Supreme Court, to which he was appointed in 1904 after service on the Massachusetts Supreme Court. In the words of Morton White, there was a "very strong cultural and intellectual tie between our most distinctive philosophy and our most distinctive philosophy of law."[57] Influenced by the English psychologist Alexander Bain and fellow club members Green and Wright, Holmes quickly grasped the significance of an empirical evolutionary approach for elucidating the role of judges in the formulation of the law.[58] This perspective seriously undercut the reliance on formal syllogistic logic that judges of Holmes's day used as the rationale for their decisions. Holmes's declaration in the opening section of his famous *The Common Law* that the "life of the law" has been experience, not logic,[59] summarized his alternative explanation of how judges arrived at their decisions. He elaborated on this position in a later address.

> ... The training of lawyers is a training in logic. The processes of analogy, discrimination, and deduction are those in which they are most at home. The language of judicial decision is mainly the language of logic. And the logical method and form flatter that longing for certainty and for repose which is in every human mind. But certainty generally is illusion, and repose is not the destiny of man. Behind the logical form lies a judgment as to the relative worth and importance of competing legislative grounds, often an inarticulate and unconscious judgment, it is true, and yet the very root and nerve of the whole proceeding. You can give any conclusion a logical form. . . .[60]

The scientific, empirical temper of the thinkers in the Metaphysical Club appears to have suggested to Holmes that the tangible human processes operating behind the rhetoric of the judicial process were more impor-

---

56 Kuklick, *op. cit.*, p. 48.
57 Morton White, *Social Thought in America* (Boston: Beacon Press, 1957), p. 62.
58 Kuklick, *op. cit.*, pp. 49–50.
59 Oliver Wendell Holmes, Jr., *The Common Law* (Boston: Little, Brown, and Company, 1881), p. 1.
60 Oliver Wendell Holmes, "The Path of the Law" in Oliver Wendell Holmes, *Collected Legal Papers* (New York: Harcourt, Brace and Company, 1921), p. 181.

tant to the formation of the law than the public posturing of the participants in the legal process. This approach ran counter to the centuries of ideology that had encased and protected the enunciation of the common law, and it was ultimately to raise the sorts of relativistic questions for judicial policy that pragmatism engendered for public policy generally.

Although pragmatic assumptions were fundamental to Holmes's conception of the judicial process, his personal philosophy remained unaffected by the implications for social reform that many pragmatists derived from their position. A close student of Hobbes and a veteran of numerous Civil War battles, Holmes saw man's lot as one of struggle and, for many, of suffering; the poor would always be part of society, for in the struggle of existence, some must lose.[61] Speaking directly to one variety of reform thought, Holmes, in his characteristically pungent fashion, conveyed the flavor of his view of reform. "[T]he notion that with socialized property, we should have women free and a piano for everybody seems . . . empty humbug."[62] For him, Spencer's application of Darwin to society was based on a far more accurate assessment of the social world than the suggestions that social cooperation would provide a better life for everyone.

Those who have seen Holmes as a reform liberal have ignored the distinction that he made between his personal beliefs and his proper role as a judge. Holmes's recognition of the force of personal biases and prejudices on a judge's decision and his understanding of the historical relativity of cultural values caused him to strive toward avoiding the interjection of his subjective values into the decisions that he made as a judge.[63] Thus, in most of his Supreme Court opinions, Holmes serves as a model of judicial restraint. In those cases involving free expression, he did not hesitate to intervene on behalf of the individual in most instances, but where social and economic policies were at issue, he often found himself in opposition to the laissez faire members of the Court who acted to prevent the implementation of legislative enactments. Holmes's stance in the latter kinds of cases placed him on the same side of Court decisions as state-interventionist liberals such as Louis D. Brandeis, when personally he had no sympathy for the reform orientation of these individuals.[64] His position was simply that, in his role as judge, it was his duty to see that the game of politics was played according to the rules

---

[61] See Beryl Harold Levy, *Our Constitution* (Port Washington, N.Y.: Kennikat Press, 1965), pp. 170–172; James Willard Hurst, *Justice Holmes on Legal History* (New York: Macmillan Company, 1964), p. 121.

[62] Quoted in Levy, *op. cit.*, p. 118.

[63] See Holmes, "Path of the Law," p. 184; also Fred V. Cahill, *Judicial Legislation* (New York: The Ronald Press, 1952), pp. 40–41.

[64] See Konefsky's discussion of this point. Samuel J. Konefsky, *The Legacy of Holmes and Brandeis* (New York: Collier Books, 1961), pp. 271–275.

and that his personal views should not be allowed to affect the outcome. In this respect, it might be argued that Holmes's attachment to democratic processes was considerably more neutral in substance than was Dewey's. Knowledge of Holmes's personal views also provides a better sense of the pervasiveness of Spencer's ideas in early twentieth-century America, for if Holmes had not acted with judicial restraint, the laissez faire majority on the Court would have been even more powerful.

Behind Holmes's conception of the proper role of a judge, there rested fairly articulate assumptions about the need for government to be able to act. There was something of social Darwinism in Holmes's treatment of the law as an instrument of the dominant powers in society at a given time.[65] For Holmes, this understanding of the law did not involve charges of exploitation in any Marxian sense but merely reflected his acceptance of the right of the majority interests in American society to have their will implemented. The beliefs of these interests might be right or wrong from a variety of ethical perspectives, but sound constitutional government required that they be channeled through the formal, legitimate procedures of government and that the ensuing legislation be recognized as valid so long as it did not threaten the procedures of democracy itself.[66] Because his primary concern was to provide a more accurate description of the judicial process, Holmes did not attempt to construct a systematic political theory, but his position on judicial restraint rather clearly indicated that he expected government to be able to act constitutionally with authority.

Ironically, Holmes's revelations that judges were mere mortals making policy from their subjective perspectives led to a movement of judicial activism that he would have disliked as much as he did the belief in the power of formal legal logic. At its base, Holmes's interpretation of the sources of the law and the forces acting in the determination of judicial policy had implications that were as relativistic as those stemming from Dewey's instrumentalism. Holmes rejected the idea that the law was a reflection of abstract principles existing somewhere as immutable certainties.

> ... It is very hard to resist the impression that there is one august corpus, to understand which clearly is the only task of any court concerned.... But there is no such body of law. The fallacy and illusion that I think exist consist in supposing that there is this outside thing to be found....[67]

Holmes believed that law is made by men for particular circumstances and that judges are to be guided in their enunciation of it by previous

---

[65] See Cahill, *op. cit.*, p. 34.

[66] Hurst, *op. cit.*, pp. 94–95.

[67] *Black and White Taxicab and Transfer Co.* v. *Brown and Yellow Taxicab and Transfer Co.*, 276 US 518 (1928), at 533.

decisions or by legislative enactments. But once it was acknowledged that judges' experiences, not some form of objective logic, were the essential component of judicial decisions, then it became possible to see the judge as another variety of policy-maker. At this point, Holmes's response was that as a judge, he had no right to substitute his view of policy for that of a duly elected legislative majority. Samuel J. Konefsky suggested that Holmes's "imperturbable confidence in the capacity of society to defy artificial meddling with its natural evolution enabled him to maintain equanimity and poise in the presence of drastic changes and grave evils...."[68] Nonetheless, his clarification of the factors that enter into a judicial decision opened the door to judicial activism, and his refusal to step through that opening in no way inhibited other judges more strongly motivated by the desire to reform society. In abandoning Holmes's general deference to the legislature, judges bent on alleviating social injustice moved the courts into the mainstream of the political policy process and subjected them to many of the partisan pressures operating in that process.

Judicial activism received much of its detailed justification from the thought of Roscoe Pound, who served as dean of Harvard Law School from 1916 to 1936 and who wrote extensively on the history of the law and on the legal process. Although he was thoroughly versed in the development of the law and the ideas of its major thinkers, Pound drew heavily on Dewey's instrumentalist position for philosophical support for his "sociological jurisprudence." "The sociological movement in jurisprudence is a movement for pragmatism as a philosophy of law; for the adjustment of principles and doctrines to the human conditions they are to govern rather than to assumed first principles...."[69] One of the major figures in American legal thought, Pound used his sociological interpretation of the law to provide a broadly based rationale for social reform powered by judicial decisions.

Pound argued that the modern era required that the judiciary recognize the need to be flexible and adaptable to changing conditions. Too many judges accepted the assumptions of the classical liberals and Spencer and remained attached to absolutist, metaphysical truths from which they believed legal decisions were derived.[70] Pound labelled this orientation "mechanical jurisprudence" and contrasted it with the or-

---

[68] Konefsky, *op. cit.*, p. 276.

[69] Quoted in Henry Steele Commager, *The American Mind* (New Haven: Yale University Press, 1950), p. 378; see also Commager's discussion on p. 380.

[70] Roscoe Pound, *The Formative Era of American Law* (Boston: Little, Brown, 1938), pp. 60–61, 210–211; Roscoe Pound, *The Spirit of the Common Law* (Boston: Beacon Press, 1963 [First published 1921]), p. 161; Roscoe Pound, *Social Control Through Law* ([n.p.]: Anchor Books, 1968 [First published in 1942]), pp. 123–124.

ganic and dynamic relationship to society that he believed the law should have.[71] Properly understood, the law was a reflection of the social forces that it guided, not an emanation from mystical absolutes detached from social facts.

Holmes had drawn attention to the actual behavior of judges in the rendering of opinions; Pound utilized Holmes's conclusions to elaborate a jurisprudence of judicial activism.[72] Judges not only made law, he declared, they were the creative element in the legal system.[73] Judges acted in the absence of legislation and applied legislation to concrete situations, some of which could not have been anticipated by a statute's authors. In essence, it was the judges who had to respond in tangible fashion to the conflicting claims of competing social interests. Their decisions dealt with real individuals in specific circumstances and had serious consequences for the parties to a suit as well as for society as a whole.[74] If the law were to be effective, judicial decisions had to continually adapt it to the changing status of social interests. Law, therefore, was sociological in its foundations, and, to be constructive forces in society, judges had to be aware of the sociological effects of their decisions.[75]

In an approach closely paralleling that of Dewey, Pound reacted to the dominance of laissez faire doctrine in the courts by expounding a jurisprudence that portrayed judges as social engineers. Judges, he argued, should strive for more than the maintenance of social equilibrium.

> ... Let us put the new point of view in terms of engineering; let us speak of a change from a political or ethical idealistic interpretation to an engineering interpretation. Let us think of the problem of the end of law in terms of a great task or great series of tasks of social engineering. ... Thus we may think of the task of the legal order as one of precluding friction and eliminating waste ...[76]

Just as Dewey depicted philosophy as instrumental to social reform, Pound posited a judiciary moving toward the same goal. Having established that judges make law, Pound then argued that this law should be consonant with social forces of reform. Obstructive judicial reliance on constitutional dogmas retained from an age of individualist thought and

---

[71] Pound, *Formative Era*, pp. 100, 110–111, 126–127.

[72] For a brief statement of Holmes's influence on Pound, see William Seal Carpenter, *Foundations of Modern Jurisprudence* (New York: Appleton-Century-Crofts, 1958), p. 220.

[73] Pound, *Formative Era*, pp. 44–45, 63.

[74] Pound, *Social Control*, p. 124; Pound *Common Law*, pp. 165, 205, 210.

[75] Pound, *Social Control*, pp. 53–54, 65–68; Pound, *Common Law*, pp. 175, 195–196, 205, 214–215.

[76] Pound, *Common Law*, pp. 195–196. Cf. "True legislation is simply the application in the sphere of social forces of the principle of invention—of objective co-ordination with a view to increase of efficiency, and preventing needless waste and friction...." John Dewey, *Essays in Experimental Logic* (Chicago: University of Chicago Press, 1916), p. 306.

behavior had to give way to a conception of government as an instrument for increasing freedom in a society that now was most constructively seen as composed of social interests.

However sophisticated Pound's sociological claims may have appeared, his understanding of the sociological data involved was, as Fred Cahill has pointed out, quite naive.[77] Pound recognized that the family, religion, and the schools were important sources of support for the law, and he voiced concern over the failure of the schools to propagate moral values effectively.[78] But he failed to recognize that his sociological jurisprudence itself seriously weakened the stability and authority of values in society, for in arguing for the socialization of the law, he was in fact advocating the politicization of the courts, an important source of social stability. Under the dicta of sociological jurisprudence, the courts lost their Holmesian role of legitimating the acts of government and became instead another arena for political conflict among those interests sufficiently knowledgeable to establish themselves as sociologically relevant.[79] Government, thus, was left without any authoritative imprimatur for its actions and moved closer to becoming totally a captive of the ensnarling demands of the continual change and adjustment that Dewey held in such high esteem.

Given Pound's status in the legal profession and the growing sympathy among intellectual circles for reform measures, it was but a matter of time until his ideas began to have influence in the courts. Both Eric Goldman and Henry Commager cite the famous Brandeis Brief in the *Muller v. Oregon*[80] case as an example of sociological jurisprudence in application.[81] In that 1908 case challenging an Oregon statute setting maximum hours of labor for women, Brandeis presented a brief on behalf of the state that contained extensive political, economic, sociological, and biological supporting data with but a few pages of formal legal precedents. Despite the general laissez faire predilections of most of the justices, Brandeis's approach was apparently sufficiently persuasive to convince a majority of them to vote to uphold the law. Certainly the Muller case had aspects of sociological jurisprudence in it. It was hardly an example of judicial social engineering, however, for the Court merely ratified reform legislation passed by the Oregon legislature.

A more recent and representative statement of the ideas of sociological jurisprudence occurred in the Supreme Court's handling of the *Brown v. Board of Education*[82] case of 1954. There, in declaring segregation in

---

[77] Cahill, *op. cit.*, pp. 80–81, 95.
[78] Pound, *Social Control*, pp. 25–26.
[79] See *ibid.*, pp. 78, 80.
[80] 208 US 412 (1908).
[81] Goldman, *op. cit.*, pp. 107–108; Commager, *op. cit.*, pp. 380–381.
[82] 347 US 483 (1954).

the public schools unconstitutional, the Court relied heavily on conclusions from the behavioral and social sciences and delved into such intangibles as group feelings and stereotypes. In succeeding decisions, the Court had to devise, or "engineer," solutions to questions about racial segregation, a process in which it is still engaged.[83] No one can reasonably argue against the outcome of the Brown case, but it is possible to suggest that the Court could have achieved the same result without opening itself to the later machinations of social scientists serving as advocates of a wide variety of social interests. There existed, at the time of the Brown decision, a clear set of constitutional precedents against segregation in education that would have served amply as a formal legal basis for outlawing that practice.[84] The Warren Court, in this instance and numerous later cases involving the poor, voters, religion, and criminal defendants, demonstrated a high level of confidence in its ability to remedy social wrongs by moving beyond the confines of formal constitutional law and dealing with them in terms of their sociological ramifications.

Toward the end of his tenure on the Court, one of the leading liberals on that body for many years, Justice Hugo Black, decried the Court's recent activism and suggested that issues before it could be dealt with constructively within narrower constitutional bounds.

> ... Our constitution was not written in the sands to be washed away by each wave of new judges blown in by each successive political wind which brings new political administrations into temporary power.... I wholly, completely, and permanently reject the so-called "activist" philosophy of some judges which leads them to construe our Constitution as meaning what they now think it should mean in the interest of "fairness and decency" as they see it.[85]

Justice Black had argued for many years that the First Amendment's protections of free expression would be effective if the Court were to abide by its unequivocal language that "Congress shall make no law ... abridging the freedom of speech, or of the press. ..."[86] Similarly, he had suggested persuasively that the privileges and immunities clause of the Fourteenth Amendment had been intended to apply the entire Bill of Rights to the states,[87] a position that would have expanded constitu-

---

[83] The Court specifically requested the attorneys to the case to research particular historical questions and to provide remedies for its consideration. See Daniel M. Berman, It Is So Ordered (New York: W. W. Norton, 1966), pp. 77–79.

[84] See Missouri ex rel. Gaines v. Canada 305 US 337 (1938); McLaurin v. Oklahoma State Regents 339 US 637 (1950); Sweatt v. Painter 339 US 629 (1950).

[85] Turner v. U.S. 396 US 398 (1970), at 426.

[86] See Craig R. Ducat, Modes of Constitutional Interpretation (St. Paul, MN.: West Publishing, 1978), p. 68.

[87] See Black's dissent in Adamson v. California 332 US 46 (1947), at 68.

tional protections more broadly and definitively than did the Warren Court and yet would have remained within the bounds of the language of the Constitution.

Obviously, judicial innovation and experimentation are not the only means by which judges may act to correct grave social problems. Indeed, such an approach may in the long run contribute significantly to the lessened effectiveness of reform-minded judges by encouraging their forays into a wide variety of issues contrived to appear as serious problems by vested interests adept at the partisan use of the social and behavioral sciences but not representative of general social interests. The result could be a public perception of judges as officials who are not effective reformers, or good politicians, or impartial adjudicators.

Compared to Hobbes's position, Dewey's instrumentalism represents the far swing of the pendulum with regard to theoretical support for governmental authority in the Anglo-American liberal tradition. Hobbes wrote clearly and candidly in support of powerful government as the means to provide security within a nation, and he regarded social interests separate from governmental authority as threats to that authority. With an eye toward the protection of property rights, Locke also wrote in support of strong government, although with him this support becomes less articulate. Bentham became a late convert to democratic government, but he never relinquished his belief in the need for firm, directive government to institute improvements in the lot of mankind. His fellow thinker, James Mill, wrote in philosophically radical terms but seems not to have considered the possibility that government and society should be led by other than the middle classes. Spencer and his American followers would have limited severely the scope of governmental activity, but where they saw government as needed, particularly in the judicial area, they envisioned it as capable of authoritative and directive action. It is true that, after Hobbes, liberal thinkers tended to focus on economic and social concerns and gave less attention to government itself, thus weakening the theoretical supports for governmental authority. Nonetheless, until Dewey, government remained an authoritative power that stood separate from and above other social forces, limited though it might be. With Dewey's instrumentalism government becomes just another tool of social interests that is evaluated by its usefulness in the here and now. Like Hobbes, Dewey saw government as judged by its consequences, but unlike the Sage of Malmesbury, Dewey failed to endow government with the authoritative legitimacy sufficient to implement coherent policy. As a tool of competing social interests evaluating its actions from every possible normative perspective, government operating within an instrumentalist framework was left without the wherewithal to become an authoritative source of values and thus of social direction and stability. Nowhere was this more aptly illustrated than in the courts, which under the effects of pragmatism lost their status of centuries in the Anglo-American tradition and potentially became but another arena of political contest.

Critics of the Primacy of Method as a Rationale for Public Policy

Throughout the twentieth century, the instrumentalist attachment to process and an optimistic view of human nature as the key ingredients for a philosophy and program of reform has come under attack. What follows is a survey of the reservations about Dewey's ideas, or their consequences, that have been raised by important American thinkers. These critics have attacked Dewey's reform philosophy and the pluralist politics that it has encouraged from a variety of perspectives, but all have been clearly within the democratic tradition. In fact, each has seen his position as contributing to a strengthening of American democracy. It is particularly significant in light of the focus of the present work that, with the possible exception of Randolph Bourne, each of the thinkers considered in this chapter saw effective, authoritative government as essential to the continued health of democratic politics. Moreover, all of them attacked the failure of the dominant form of American liberalism to provide a theoretical basis for government that would enable coherent policy formulation and implementation.

Randolph Bourne

The crisis of values engendered by the passions and destruction unleashed by World War I produced an acute critique of the problems inherent in Dewey's philosophy by one of his former students and devotees. With America's entry into the war, Randolph Bourne, a complex thinker, accomplished writer, and in many ways tragic figure, turned from praising the father of instrumentalism to questioning how the proponent of such humane ideas could support the rabid emotionalism of a warring nation. He concluded that the instrumentalist position was incapable of providing constructive guidance to real human beings in an actual crisis. The philosophy that billed itself as dealing with the practical questions of life had failed when put to a serious test.

Bourne charged that, in the face of calls for bold actions and emphatic beliefs, the instrumentalist as a person could not tolerate the uncertainty involved in his philosophical stance of value neutrality. Thus, American intellectuals quickly shed their responsibilities as moral leaders and plunged into the certainty and social acceptance provided by their support of the war effort.[1] Leaders such as Dewey may have believed that, through their support, they could have some control over the direction of the war and that, through the imposition of democratic ideals on the vanquished, the war would ultimately have a constructive effect. But they were to be sadly mistaken, declared Bourne, for the forces of war were far too powerful to be influenced by intellectuals guided by instrumentalist precepts. It was only naive self-righteousness that led the instrumentalists to look toward making the world safe for democracy when domestically America still provided ample opportunity for liberal reforms.[2] The real enemy, Bourne insisted, was war, not Germany, and the normative failings of instrumentalism prevented its adherents from making this distinction.[3]

Emphasis on process and on techniques of adjustment and adaptation had rendered the instrumentalists valuationally impotent. The young instrumentalists had found a certain contentment during the war, for they were able to concentrate on the problems of sending the nation into war and could derive satisfaction from the technical efficiency that they had achieved.[4] But, from Bourne's point of view, this focus on the specific constituted the essential difficulty in instrumentalism. The wartime experience had shown that it was a philosophy incapable of transcending the dislocations of the moment. In times of crisis, it left its disciples and Americans generally at the mercy of those individuals who were certain of their beliefs and not afraid to act on them.[5] Thus, the war effort had quickly fallen into the hands of the "professional patriots, sensational editors, [and] archaic radicals."[6]

The war had brought the inadequacies of instrumentalism to the fore by demonstrating that it was in fact a benign philosophy dependent on a

---

[1] Randolph Bourne, "War and the Intellectuals" in Randolph Bourne, *War and the Intellectuals: Essays, 1915–1919.* Edited with introduction by Carl Resek (New York: Harper and Row, 1964), pp. 11–12; Randolph Bourne, "Below the Battle" in *ibid.*, p. 17.

[2] Randolph Bourne, "Twilight of Idols" in *ibid.*, p. 57; Randolph Bourne, "A War Diary" in *ibid.*, pp. 39–40.

[3] Bourne, "War," p. 13.

[4] Bourne, "Twilight," pp. 58–62.

[5] *Ibid.*, p. 61.

[6] *Ibid.*, p. 60.

reservoir of good will. In times of peace and prosperity, it worked reasonably well as a guide to action because, in Bourne's words, "we had our own private utopias and the means fell into place."[7] Despite their protestations to the contrary, the instrumentalists depended very heavily on the values behind the reformers' optimistic assumptions about social cooperation. Dewey's persistent refusal to proffer substantive values for his philosophical method reflected his blindness to the possibility that a particular valuational context was essential to the successful functioning of his ideas. This lack of value articulation fit well with the pluralistic nature of American society but left his disciples defenseless against the "raw-nerved, irrational, uncreative" forces encouraged by the hysteria of wartime.[8]

Unfortunately for American culture, Bourne died a young man in the flu epidemic of 1918, just a few days before the signing of the armistice ending the war. His contributions to the intellectual dialogue of his time are to be found in the articles that he wrote for a variety of New York magazines between 1910 and 1918. He examined a wide range of cultural topics but never produced a systematic work on politics, although his untimely death left uncompleted a manuscript on the state. Yet, better than anyone else of his time, Bourne pinpointed some of the flaws inherent in what was rapidly becoming America's dominant philosophy of reform. Some might charge that his criticisms of instrumentalism were context specific and that, due perhaps to the personal vacillations of some of its leading spokesmen during World War I, it appeared more vulnerable to exploitation than it was. Such a charge would have more force were it not for the tragic experience of a recent President who attempted to establish a "Great Society" for all Americans but also found his good intentions dashed by the emotions unleashed by another, even more frustrating war.

Herbert Croly

Insightful as his criticisms of instrumentalism were, Bourne offered little that was positive or systematic in the way of an alternative. In fact, something of the sort had already been provided by Herbert Croly's *The Promise of American Life* published in 1909, the year that Bourne had entered Columbia University. Immensely popular for a time, *The Promise of American Life* spoke directly to the need for Americans to begin to think in terms of consciously directing their destinies through the articulation of a national spirit embodied in effective government.[9] Americans

---

[7] *Ibid.*, also p. 55.
[8] *Ibid.*, p. 54.
[9] Herbert Croly, *The Promise of American Life.* Introduction by Charles Forcey (New York: E. P. Dutton, 1963 [First published in 1909]), pp. 18, 22.

had been too fortunate for their own good, Croly argued. They had been able "to slide down hill into the valley of fulfillment"[10] and thus had contented themselves with believing that the American political system, unexamined though it was, was the best of all possible approaches to government. Unfortunately, America's political innocence was now face-to-face with the harsh realities posed by rapid industrialization and the closing of the frontier.

Croly was unimpressed with the sophistication of American attempts at social reform. The problem was that the nation had no guiding social ideal by which interests could be judged and which could serve as a goal for action. Without such an ideal, "good" causes were essentially as narrow, partisan, and subjective as "bad" causes. In this respect, the moralistic rhetoric of the reformers was often, at its base, as vulnerable to criticism as the abuses that it was used to attack.[11] Effective reform required a dynamic national government that could implement national ideals. To this end, Croly proposed a regeneration of the American national spirit through the wedding of Hamiltonian methods to Jeffersonian ends. Americans should recognize that the values of liberty and equality preached by Jefferson could not, by themselves, provide the momentum for continued progress in an industrial age. Instead, the best prospects for progress were to be found under a powerful national government in the Hamiltonian sense that was guided by Jeffersonian values with re-spect to individuals.[12] Such a combination would require self-denial and discipline on the part of the nation's people, but Croly expected their leaders to persuade them that American democracy could not achieve its full potential if government were to respond to every whim of the major-ity.[13] It was incumbent on the nation's leaders to project a sense of na-tional purpose, a social ideal that would attract support from the people.

> ... The common citizen can become something of a saint and something of a hero ... by the sincere and enthusiastic imitation of heroes and saints, and whether or not he will ever come to such imitation will depend upon the ability of his exceptional fellow-countrymen to offer him acceptable examples of heroism and saintliness.[14]

Obviously, Croly did not recoil from values and ideals. To him, they were essential to effective democratic government. "The principle of democ-racy *is* virtue," he asserted, and, in his mind, full realization of this principle required a government able to act firmly and authoritatively.[15]

---

[10] *Ibid.*, p. 17.
[11] *Ibid.*, pp. 138–139, 143–146, 150.
[12] *Ibid.*, pp. 29, 43, 51, 153, 214.
[13] *Ibid.*, p. 33.
[14] *Ibid.*, p. 454.
[15] *Ibid.*

In light of the current state of American politics, Croly's early effort retains its importance as a frank and reasoned statement for powerful government and for the value of national ideals. It stands as a plea for reform with direction and permanence that has seldom been equalled in the depth of its analysis of the American political culture. Croly's statement of national purpose made a tremendous impression on Theodore Roosevelt, and much of the "New Nationalism" propounded by Roosevelt in his 1912 Bull Moose bid for the presidency can be found in *The Promise of American Life*. However, the ideas advocated by Croly did not retain their popularity after Wilson's victory in that election. The specter of powerful government and elitism in Croly's work was unpalatable to many American intellectuals, and Croly himself later modified his views in favor of a greater degree of participatory democracy. Nonetheless, Croly's early position supporting governmental authority was to be echoed for much of the twentieth century in the works of Walter Lippmann, who as a young man had been sought out and hired by Croly to write for the *New Republic*.[16]

Walter Lippmann

Published in 1955, Lippmann's *Essays in the Public Philosophy* summarizes four decades of experience in public life and reflection on the meaning of liberal democracy. The *Public Philosophy* is a short book, but its 138 pages contain an articulate, cogent statement of democratic thought that contrasts markedly with the egalitarian, optimistic assertions of Dewey. Lippmann made no claims to be "scientific" in his approach. His position was based on what might be termed a "common-sense" understanding of the way that American politics worked and on an acceptance of the importance of substantive values.

From Lippmann's perspective, liberal democracies were floundering because they had lost the capacity to govern.[17] He agreed with Croly that, in this country, the peace and prosperity following the Civil War had led most Americans to believe that weak government was the best kind of government and that this position had discouraged inquiry into the institutional forms required for the effective exercise of governmental authority.[18] The failings of other western democracies in this respect were reflected in the institutional degeneration of their governments under the crisis of World War I. Instead of continuing to lead their nations during this period, the western governments faltered in their

---

[16] See Ronald Steel, *Walter Lippmann and the American Century* (New York: Vintage Books, 1981), pp. 59–63.

[17] Walter Lippmann, *The Public Philosophy* (New York: Mentor Books, 1956 [First published in 1955]), pp. 29, 53–54.

[18] *Ibid.*, pp. 15–16.

confidence and turned to the masses for reinforcement and direction. The resulting institutional "derangement" between the governors and the governed had had disastrous consequences for the ensuing short-lived peace and, after World War II, had rendered these democracies too weak to deal successfully with "mounting disorder" on the one hand and threats from "counter-revolutionary" forces favoring authoritarian government on the other.[19]

In Lippmann's opinion, the institutional disrepair of the western democracies was best illustrated by the debilitating limits that a misplaced trust in the wisdom of the people had placed on the executive and judicial powers.[20] Lippmann shared none of the optimistic enthusiasm for the common citizen that permeated Dewey's works. If one examines the masses stripped of their adornment of liberal rhetoric, he must conclude, Lippmann argued, that they are simply incapable of participating in the formulation of policy in any continuing or direct fashion. Returning to a model first used in his book *Public Opinion*, Lippmann described the average citizen's conception of the political world as limited to images in his head that failed to portray the detail and complexity of issues. Democratic systems should recognize the limitations of the voters and restrict their input to judgment at the polls.[21] Drawing on his knowledge of American history, Lippmann was convinced that, at critical junctures in America's past, public opinion had been "destructively wrong" about the direction to be taken. The Jacksonian democratic creed had engendered a "Jacobin" belief in the right of public political participation that had hamstrung the executive power by tying it to the whims of the people.[22] The executive, Lippmann declared, had lost its "material and ethereal powers."[23] The resulting impotence posed a serious threat to individual liberty and democracy itself.

Fundamentally, Americans needed a change in the terms in which political discussion occurred. The claims of the dominant "positivist" thinkers had led to a privatization of morals and to an America in which the individual was without an "authentic world."[24] These thinkers depicted the public as an aggregation of discrete individuals, when a far more constructive and accurate view would be Burkean in nature. In the Burkean paradigm, the individual constituted an organic part of society, and the contemporary community was but the latest stage in a long tradition and served as the repository of the interests of future generations.

---

[19] *Ibid.*, pp. 12, 17–18, 32, 53.
[20] *Ibid.*, p. 29.
[21] *Ibid.*, pp. 27, 39, 46, 73.
[22] *Ibid.*, pp. 19, 23–24, 56, 61.
[23] *Ibid.*, pp. 18, 48, 50.
[24] *Ibid.*, pp. 75, 78–79, 85–87, 137.

Viewed from this perspective, the interests of the public could never be wholly defined on election day, and, in fact, current opinion could quite simply be wrong as to the best interests of the total community.[25]

Taking a position similar to that of Croly almost fifty years earlier, Lippmann concluded that effective democratic government required a public philosophy based on the traditions of civility drawn from the history of western civilization. The public philosophy would be a form of natural law consisting of those norms that rational individuals who are fully informed would accept. These included recognition of the importance of law in society and a belief that rational individuals acting with good will can reach constructive agreement on issues.[26] Although he believed that the precepts of the public philosophy had been essential elements of the western tradition since at least the time of Socrates, Lippmann recognized that the discipline of public desires required by it would render it especially unpopular in an era when positivists assiduously propagated the illusion of the citizen's political omnipotence. Thus, Lippmann urged America's intellectuals to accept the public philosophy and to disseminate it among the citizenry.[27]

Lippmann saw clearly that democracy can not survive without a belief system that has the support of its citizens, allows government to act to protect them, and provides reasonably objective standards of progress and of right and wrong. Philosophical systems such as Dewey's were inadequate for this task because their focus on the immediate, coupled with their erroneous assumptions about the political capabilities of individuals, destroyed their ability to support effective political authority. Lippmann's critique of the liberalism of his day was perceptive and suggested the possibility of an alternative approach to democratic politics. Despite his insight, however, Lippmann could not be said to have dealt adequately with the problem of implementing such an alternative, for, in his call to intellectuals to accept the public philosophy, he was in effect walking unarmed into the camp of the enemy.

Reinhold Niebuhr

The prominent Protestant theologian Reinhold Niebuhr agreed with Lippmann that democracy faced serious internal threats stemming from the failure or unwillingness of liberals to re-examine their assumptions about human nature. Like Lippmann, he was especially concerned by

---

[25] *Ibid.*, pp. 34–35, 81, 125.

[26] *Ibid.*, pp. 75, 81–105, 123.

[27] *Ibid.*, pp. 104, 124. The flavor of the response of the instrumentalists to Lippmann's position was probably reflected in Dewey's reaction to Lippmann's earlier *The Good Society*. Dewey thought the book a form of "encouragement" and "support" for "reactionaries." Quoted in Steel, *op. cit.*, p. 325.

the rise of totalitarian regimes during the 1930s and 1940s. In the face of these movements, modern liberals continued their attachment to the "touching faith" of their seventeenth-century progenitors that there existed a natural harmony between individual self-interest and community well-being.[28] But, Niebuhr cautioned, the "illusions and sentimentalities of the Age of Reason" could no longer serve as the basis for democracy, for they had "not squared with the facts of history."[29] These liberal superficialities were innocuous during an era of burgeoning economic development and relative social stability, but now they could lead democracy into disaster.[30] Although it is a "permanently valid" form of political and social organization,[31] democracy's survival requires an accurate assessment of individuals and their relations with each other.

Niebuhr rejected the secularism of modern liberalism and turned to the insights of Christianity for a firmer conceptual basis to democratic ideas and practices. To him, Christianity's depiction of human nature was more accurate than the optimistic artificiality constructed by liberalism. Moreover, in contrast to secular ends, which he saw as ultimately stultifying to human endeavor, spiritual values were necessary for community well-being and social progress. Christian doctrine was based on centuries of experience with mankind, yet it remained sufficiently flexible to provide a constructive framework for modern democracy. In a time of increasing secularism, the continued relevance of Niebuhr's ideas stands as a testament to the power of his intellectual and religious insights.

The fundamental difficulty with the approach of modern liberals, as well as that of the utopian Marxists, Niebuhr asserted, was the refusal to acknowledge the validity of the Christian doctrine of original sin. Liberals seemed to believe that given a bit more time and greater educational efforts social conflicts would be peaceably resolved.[32] But the "dream of perpetual peace and brotherhood," while of some value as a social ideal, was beyond attainment due to the ineradicable existence of original sin, or self-pride, in the human psyche.[33] Niebuhr recognized that the forces of inordinate pride could often be controlled at the individual level, but he argued that within groups of individuals these forces have a cumulative impact that makes organizations and nations inherently less moral than most individuals, a position reflected in the title of one of his early

---

[28] Reinhold Niebuhr, *The Children of Light and the Children of Darkness* (New York: Charles Scribner's Sons, 1960 [First published in 1944]), p. 7.

[29] *Ibid.*, p. 40.

[30] *Ibid.*, pp. 16, 40; Reinhold Niebuhr, *Moral Man and Immoral Society* (New York: Charles Scribner's Sons, 1960 [First published in 1932]), p. 22.

[31] Niebuhr, *Children*, pp. 3, 48–49, 63–64.

[32] Niebuhr, *Moral Man*, pp. xiii-xiv, xxiii.

[33] *Ibid.*, pp. xiii-xiv, 21.

works, *Moral Man and Immoral Society* (1932). Later, in his *The Children of Light and the Children of Darkness* (1944), Niebuhr urged liberals to draw on the wisdom that the forces of oppression—the children of darkness—had shown in their appreciation of the power of self-pride in human affairs. If they were to utilize this wisdom, liberals would understand that coercion is an essential and thoroughly justifiable method for maintaining social stability.[34] It is, in fact, necessary for the establishment of that balance between the demands of liberty and order that must be the foundation for effective democratic government.

Niebuhr argued that the liberals' faith in human rationality was misplaced. It ignored the dangers posed to social stability by self-interest[35] and led to confusions about the function of non-rational forces in society. Infatuated with science and the scientific method, liberals had blurred the important distinctions between the physical sciences and social relations and thus had denigrated the contribution of myth and symbolism to social morale.[36] This inability of the liberal intellectuals to fathom the role of emotionally laden ideas had contributed heavily to their sorry performance during World War I. The politician, Niebuhr remarked, knew that he was manipulating symbols and ideas to produce national unity in a crisis. The liberal intellectuals, however, had been easily drawn into believing in the innate validity of the moralistic universals that were hyped for the war effort, and, in turning their tools of rationality toward justifying the war, they had become "the worst liars of war-time."[37]

Much of Niebuhr's invective against the liberals was directed at Dewey and his disciples. In the introduction to *Moral Man and Immoral Society*, Niebuhr quoted Dewey at length, taking him to task for the use of ambiguous platitudes and a lack of clear thinking. Dewey's insistence that the source of social problems was individual ignorance revealed his biases as an educator. The application of reason and education to social issues would, of course, aid in social improvement, but no amount of education and rational persuasion could offset the destabilizing effects of the selfish drives propelled by the human ego. The idea of social cohesion without coercion was simply a pedagogical pipe dream on Dewey's part that, clothed in optimism and ambiguities, had been foisted on the public.[38]

Similarly, Niebuhr attacked the liberals' reliance on experts for the solutions to social problems. With or without experts, the underlying forces of irrationality would continue to threaten democratic society. Policy, Niebuhr declared, is the result of the machinations of interests

---

[34] *Ibid.*, pp. xii, 4, 6; Niebuhr, *Children*, pp. xii, xv, 18, 67.
[35] Niebuhr, *Moral Man*, p. xiv; Niebuhr, *Children*, pp. xii, 18, 24.
[36] Niebuhr, *Moral Man*, pp. xiv, 65, 81, 199.
[37] *Ibid.*, p. 97.
[38] *Ibid.*, pp. xv, 3, 6; Niebuhr, *Children*, p. 67.

pursuing their selfish ends, and "the expert is quite capable of giving any previously determined tendency both rational justification and efficient detailed application. . . ."[39] Here, Niebuhr saw clearly what later students of the policy process such as Charles Lindblom have demonstrated, namely, that despite all of the logical paraphernalia invoked by the policy analyst, somewhere behind his or her efforts lie value assumptions that cannot be defended on strictly rational grounds.[40]

Niebuhr believed that democracy should be seen as a means for achieving "proximate solutions for insoluble problems."[41] Creative change required that even the fundamental beliefs of a culture must be open to questioning. "A society which exempts ultimate principles from criticisms will find difficulty in dealing with the historical forces which have appropriated these truths as their special possession."[42] Ideals can be important stimuli for human striving, but, seen as absolutes guiding public policy in concrete situations, they too often shut "the gates of mercy on mankind."[43] Somewhat surprisingly, Niebuhr charged that the liberal followers of Dewey were inflexible on important points, and in doing so he attacked them at perhaps their strongest point, their stance of value neutrality. The universalistic claims of the contemporary liberal bourgeois secular faith were "pathetic" in the face of evidence that they were but the "peculiar convictions of a special class" dominant at a particular time in the West.[44] Furthermore, the narrow secularism of the modern liberals obstructed continued human progress. No society, asserted Niebuhr, is so good that it can claim to be "the final end of human existence" now or in the future. The vital essence of man's nature is his capacity to transcend the immediate social context and to ask questions which all of human history is unable to answer and which demonstrate his innate religious capacity.[45] Thus, the secular finality of the nominalistic philosophy of modern liberalism rendered it unacceptable as a foundation for creative democracy.

As Niebuhr interpreted it, the Christian tradition contributed to more effective democratic government not only through its candid appraisal of human nature but also through its teaching of humility in response to the imperfections of the human condition. Toleration and humility are essential components of a viable democratic process, Niebuhr argued,

---

[39] Niebuhr, *Moral Man*, p. 214.
[40] See Charles Lindblom, *The Policy-Making Process* (Englewood Cliffs, N.J.: Prentice-Hall, 1968), pp. 16–17.
[41] Niebuhr, *Children*, p. 118.
[42] *Ibid.*, p. 75.
[43] Niebuhr, *Moral Man*, p. 199.
[44] Niebuhr, *Children*, p. 131.
[45] *Ibid.*, pp. 71, 79, 84–85, 132–133, see also Niebuhr's citation of Dewey's *A Common Faith* at p. 129.

for he saw groups and individuals with absolute attachments to "relative political ends" as serious threats to the stability and openness of a democratic system.[46] Democracy benefited from the orientation toward compromise that was engendered by individuals with a sense of humility and an understanding of man's imperfections. For Niebuhr, there were no absolute standards. Certainly Christianity could not claim to provide them. It could, however, offer a realistic perspective on the individual and his role in society. In this respect, Christian theology provided a much firmer basis for democratic government than did secular liberalism and, in this manner, it contributed significantly to the survival chances of that form of government.

Theodore Lowi

Perhaps the most convincing and thorough treatment of the practical political ramifications of liberalism's failure to examine the theoretical bases for governmental authority has been presented by the political scientist Theodore J. Lowi. In his *The End of Liberalism*, Lowi has done an outstanding job of demonstrating how theoretical flaws in political ideas can translate into governmental impotence. He argues that liberals, and political scientists in particular, have for the past forty years refused to examine the forms of authority and have tried to ignore the issue by burying their heads in the sands of process and methodology.[47] In his opinion, current American national government is really part of a second republic that had its origins in the New Deal's acceptance of activist government.[48] This present form of American politics suffered a crisis of public authority in the early 1960s when organized interests were largely successful in undermining the powers of the legal institutions of government.[49] The result has been the dominance of what he labels "interest-group" liberalism and a corresponding decline in government legitimacy and authority.[50]

In *The End of Liberalism*, Lowi does not mention thinkers such as Dewey or Pound, but his analysis serves exceptionally well as a critique of the consequences of the ideas of the instrumentalists. Clearly, Lowi has concluded that philosophical altruism and good intentions in the cause of reform have not been sufficient to produce effective government. As Lowi sees the present state of affairs, organized interests have be-

---

[46] *Ibid.*, pp. 82, 135, 151–152.

[47] Theodore J. Lowi, *The End of Liberalism* (Second edition; New York: W. W. Norton, 1979), pp. xv-xvi.

[48] *Ibid.*, pp. xii, xv.

[49] *Ibid.*, pp. xi, 50, 271. The second edition of *The End of Liberalism* is subtitled *The Second Republic of the United States*. The first edition published in 1969 carried the subtitle *Ideology, Policy and the Crisis of Public Authority.*

[50] *Ibid.*, pp. xi, 36, 50–51, 126.

come the purveyors and definers of social virtue.[51] The equilibrium that self-interested groups negotiate among themselves is accepted by interest-group liberalism as the public interest.[52] The political process operates not within the framework of a national interest drawing on general moral principles but in terms of how much each interest can appropriate for itself from the country's wealth. Those unorganized and without influence are excluded from the policy process, and those within it are often misled by the materialistic criteria pervading it. Thus, Lowi charges that blacks sold out for the immediate and short-lived economic rewards of a War on Poverty when they should have been thinking and acting in terms of broader and more permanent social goals.[53]

An underlying assumption of interest-group liberalism has been its rejection of formalisms as standards for action or judgment.[54] The liberal leader finds his or her ambivalence toward the use of coercion resolved by allowing the process of group interaction to serve as the basis and standard for policy determination. But, Lowi argues, this deference to the group process seriously weakens the ability of government to act, for one of the defining attributes of government is its right to use force.[55] Within the context of interest-group liberalism, government has lost its power to promulgate authoritative standards because it is understood that government rules will be modified by informal bargaining among the interests affected. In fact, Congress now routinely delegates vast amounts of discretion to the executive branch with the intention of allowing the agencies and their clientele groups to negotiate substantive policy in their areas.[56] The result has been that public officials at the national level have, in effect, ceased to govern. Liberal jurisprudence has become "a contradiction in terms." The inability of public officials to deal specifically and definitively with issues has led to a "governmental and social pathology" which has left government impotent and without legitimacy.[57] The ideology of interest-group liberalism, in its justification of informal group interaction as the source of public policy, has failed the nation by depriving its political leaders of a coherent, consistent rationale for acting.

As an alternative to interest-group liberalism, Lowi offers juridical democracy. Juridical democracy would be characterized by governmental rules that could be effectively enforced by public officials themselves. The law would be enforced as it was written and would specify standards

---

[51] *Ibid.*, p. 36.
[52] *Ibid.*, pp. 43, 51.
[53] *Ibid.*, pp. 57–58, 235, 293–297.
[54] *Ibid.*, pp. xvi, 50, 63.
[55] *Ibid.*, pp. 37, 56.
[56] *Ibid.*, pp. xii, 33, 60.
[57] *Ibid.*, pp. 92–93.

of right and wrong conduct.[58] Thus, Lowi introduces the formalism of effective governmental laws as the route to the recovery of government's legitimacy and authority. Of particular interest to students of public law is his suggestion that the Roosevelt victory over the Supreme Court in 1937 has been misconceived by most scholars and pundits. Lowi's interpretation of the affair is that for daring to insist that clear standards be contained in legislation, as for example in its opinion in the Schechter Case,[59] the Court was attacked and maimed by the proponents of interest-group liberalism.[60] The Court remains, however, an important element in the resolution of the present political chaos, for it retains the power to insist that Congress return to the incorporation of definitive standards in its legislation. Unlike the other thinkers treated in this chapter, Lowi has not been content to rely on persuasion and the good offices of America's intellectual leaders as the means for enhancing governmental authority and overcoming group self-interest. Instead, by suggesting that the Court intervene to insist on the substantive legislative standards necessary for juridical democracy, Lowi has wisely called on the one institution capable of providing practical leadership that could distance itself from the vortex of group interaction.

Lowi has recognized the parallels between interest-group liberalism and classical economics. He notes that, with the passing of government acceptance of laissez faire economics, the political arena has in turn become the scene of laissez faire interest-group politics.[61] He argues that the wide range of interest-group activity that has developed has effectively freed government from being the captive of a particular class or interest but concludes that this development has also had the effect of leaving government without external support by divorcing it from its socioeconomic context.[62] Certainly interest-group politics has diffused power in society to the extent that government now must search for support among constantly shifting alignments of interests. However, a more accurate statement of the contemporary political process might be drawn from the insight shown by Lowi's remark that the political pluralism of today is really pluralism sponsored to a great extent by government.[63] Thus, it would seem more plausible to argue that, instead of having become separated from its socioeconomic context, government has been dismembered by the interests that have attached themselves to particular segments of it.[64]

---

[58] *Ibid.*, pp. xvi, 293, 304.
[59] *Schechter Poultry Corp.* v. *U.S.* 295 US 495 (1935).
[60] Lowi, *op. cit.*, p. 102.
[61] *Ibid.*, p. 22.
[62] *Ibid.*, pp. 34, 36.
[63] *Ibid.*, pp. 33, 60.
[64] On this point, E.E. Schattschneider's view of American government as the

Lowi's interpretation adds significantly to an understanding of the development of the liberal attitude toward governmental authority, but appeals to government have already begun to extend beyond the economic framework within which Lowi wrote. In the next chapter, it will be suggested that the liberal conception of government now encompasses not only claims on the economic largesse of the public but also demands for official support for such social issues as sexual styles, particular interpretations of the Bible, and standards of acceptable use of the English vocabulary. These expectations of government conveyed through the processes of interest-group liberalism have engendered a value relativism in the American social order that ultimately threatens the basis of democratic constitutionalism and whatever remains of liberalism itself. Nonetheless, Lowi's critique of contemporary liberal politics stands as an important articulation of an unease about the direction of American politics that has concerned many. As political developments are making increasingly clear, much of this uncertainty can be traced to the refusal of the reform liberals to re-examine their assumptions about human nature and the status of government. In Lowi's work, the naive assumptions of reform liberal thought and the failure of liberalism in general to provide theoretical support for government authority surface as serious flaws in the liberal conception of politics.

The Strange Persistence of Liberal Innocence in the Forest of American Politics

Despite the appearance throughout the twentieth century of perceptive critiques of the assumptions and political manifestations of reform liberalism, the ideas of John Dewey continue their dominance of the American political psyche. One might argue that Dewey's influence has been due to the combination of his peculiar status in American education and the demogogic force of his claims about man's innate rationality and the scientific nature of his approach. Certainly his widespread appeal cannot be attributed to his writing style, which, in comparison with that of the thinkers examined in this chapter, might charitably be characterized as turgid. Nor in light of his critics' attacks can his political philosophy be defended on the grounds of unassailable logical rigor. Dewey did have an important advantage over most of his critics, however, in that he served as a recognized scholar at major American universities that turned out graduate students who would in turn spread the philosophy of reform. Further, he involved himself directly in shaping the approaches that should be taken in the secondary and elementary schools

---

"socialization of conflict" is especially relevant. See E. E. Schattschneider, *The Semisovereign People* (New York: Holt, Rinehart and Winston, 1960), pp. 13–18.

of the nation.[65] In these respects, Dewey had a tremendous impact on the institutions of education throughout the country, and quite probably after the 1930s his ideas in one form or another reached, at some point, every individual who attended American schools for any length of time. Additionally, although Dewey saw himself as the spokesman for reform, his ideas were in fact comforting statements of what Americans wanted to believe. His critics might point out that a democratic society needed some form of direction, but most Americans saw no need to go beyond the pleasant, egalitarian assurances that Dewey offered them.

Persuasive as the foregoing argument for Dewey's influence may appear, it pales in comparison to the support that Dewey's ideas have received from the activities of vested interests in America. The reform liberals' deference to process, their refusal to advocate specific standards of right and wrong, and their unwillingness to admit the power of self-interest in society have, in effect, provided *carte blanche* to organized interests. The leaders of these interests are also important molders of opinion, and to rephrase a point made by Niebuhr, they have not hesitated to exploit the political naivete of the liberals. In what must be one of the major intellectual ironies of the twentieth century, the philosophy of reform liberalism has become the stalking horse of vested political forces. Because the internal mechanisms of organized interests prevent their spokesmen from moving much beyond the self-seeking needs of their members, the dominance of these forces politically has lowered the moral tone of political debate and swept considerations of long-term national interest from the political arena. The intellectual critics of interest-group liberalism have served and will continue to serve an important role in suggesting that there are serious difficulties with such a limited approach to politics. But until conditions conspire to discredit the assumptions of reform liberalism, they will remain outside the moving forces of American politics.

---

[65] For an indication of Dewey's influence in American education, see Lawrence A. Cremin, *The Transformation of the School* (New York: Vintage, 1961).

Contemporary Manifestations of Reform Liberal Ideology

T he reservations about reform liberalism's political ideas voiced by its critics have been reflected in the practices and trends of contemporary American political processes. Denied the direction provided by substantive social norms, American government has been left at the mercy of interests adept at manipulating the political process on behalf of their particular, and often peculiar, self-serving values. The value neutrality of the reform liberals, combined with their optimistic, egalitarian assumptions about human nature, has fostered a kind of interest-group free-for-all or, in Burke's words, a "national gaming table" where the spoils of government accrue to the masters of technique and procedure. The scope of this competition has widened dramatically in the last two decades to the point where virtually every aspect of human existence in this country has become contested politically. The result has been a situation where important values of the reform liberals themselves have been seriously undermined. Science, the underlying source of value stability for the liberals, today is rapidly becoming but another weapon to be wielded by competing interests, and the poor and disadvantaged have found that often they are more important as fodder for the rhetoric of political conflict than as individuals in need. Finally, the unarticulated forms of social control that functioned passably well during the latter nineteenth and early twentieth centuries have been significantly diluted. The politicization of what were once regarded as purely personal beliefs and problems has opened almost every facet of an inherently pluralistic society to cynical, questioning debate that is characterized by a level of personal involvement and intensity that appears to be considerably more accentuated than that accompanying earlier debates, which dealt primarily with economic issues.

The Contribution of Sociological Theory to Value Manipulation

The extension of the cloak of political legitimacy to an ever increasing range of social interests has occurred in a context of cultural relativism that has been encouraged by the stances taken by that part of the academic community which focuses on individual and social behavior, and one of the best examples of this effect is provided by the discipline of sociology. American sociologists have devoted a tremendous amount of effort to the study of deviance in society, and, in their attempts to understand deviant behavior, they have pointed the way toward rationalizing away its unacceptability.[1] Specifically, their increasing willingness to see deviance as socially defined has been paralleled by the efforts of a variety of interests espousing peculiar behavior of one sort or another to organize to change the social stigma attached to their beliefs. Inevitably, an important goal of these groups must be the achievement of sufficient political influence to remove legal barriers to their activities.

Like many other academic disciplines, sociology in the twentieth century has been significantly influenced by Dewey's ideas, and nowhere is this more apparent than in the thought of one of the most influential American sociologists, George Herbert Mead, who can justifiably be seen as founder of the symbolic interactionist school of sociological thinking.[2] In 1891, Mead returned from study in Germany to take a position at the University of Michigan, where he and Dewey soon became close friends. When Dewey left for the University of Chicago, Mead followed him. He was to stay at Chicago until his death in 1931, and, although Dewey left years earlier, they remained close friends.[3] The intellectual interchange between Dewey and Mead must have resulted in considerable reciprocity of influence, and it may be unfair to describe Dewey as the dominant thinker, although it is true that Dewey published prolifically while Mead had very little appear in print during his lifetime. Like Dewey and many other reform liberals, Mead reacted strongly against the formalistic philosophical positions of the nineteenth century. His ideas fit within the intellectual context created by Darwin's *Origin of Species* in their empha-

---

[1] David Matza, *Becoming Deviant* (Englewood Cliffs, N.J.: Prentice-Hall, 1969) gives an excellent overview of various sociological approaches to deviance. See also Alexander Liazos, "The Poverty of Sociology of Deviance: Nuts, Sluts, and Perverts," *Social Problems*, XX (Summer, 1972). pp. 103–120.

[2] A recent work, J. David Lewis and Richard L. Smith, *American Sociology and Pragmatism* (Chicago: University of Chicago, 1980), has argued against the current assessment of the extent of Mead's influence. See, however, the criticism of Lewis and Smith's position in *Contemporary Sociology*. Eugene Rochberg-Hilton, "The Real Relationship Between Pragmatism and Chicago Sociology," *Contemporary Sociology*, XI (March, 1982), pp. 140–142.

[3] Lewis A. Coser, *Masters of Sociological Thought* (New York: Harcourt Brace Jovanovich, 1971), p. 343; David L. Miller, *George Herbert Mead* (Austin, TX: University of Texas, 1973), p. xxxvii.

sis on process and on a naturalistic view of mind. In this respect also, it is clear that Dewey's revision of the reflex arc concept in psychology was one of the most important early influences on Mead's thought.[4] Dewey's rejection of the stimulus-response dichotomy as artificial and his insistence that the reflex arc was meaningful only when seen as part of a larger cyclical process of continuous formulation and reformulation,[5] in its essentials, anticipated remarkably well the symbolic interactionist view of the relationship between the individual and society.

For Mead, as for Dewey, each personality develops from the human organism's interaction with its social environment. Consciousness, or mind, can not exist independent of or prior to society.[6] Those with whom the individual communicates are largely determinative in fashioning how a person thinks and acts and are the source of reason and values in the individual.[7] The individual's interaction with society generates social responses to himself or herself, which Mead labelled the "generalized other."[8] These responses the individual incorporates into his perspective on the world, and they become, in effect, his sense of identity and meaning.[9] Mead noted that the formation of an individual's consciousness was triadic.[10] It involved stimulus, response, and incorporation by the individual of the response in a process similar to the dialectical approach of the Hegelian school of thought.

The importance of Mead's ideas for contemporary sociology and for an understanding of the context and techniques of interest group politics derives from the power that they convey to the social environment for the creation of individual meaning. Under Mead's system, values can not be derived from within an individualized mind or from metaphysical universals but are functions of the social context within which the individual interacts. Especially influential in this respect is language, which Mead saw as a primary form of communication and thus as an exceptionally important source of meaning for the individual.[11] Mead himself did not focus on the manipulation of language for the purpose of refashioning values, but his ideas certainly suggested that this was possible.[12]

---

[4] Miller, *op. cit.*, pp. xvi, xxv-xxvi, xxviii.

[5] John Dewey, "The Reflex Arc Concept in Psychology" in *The Early Works of John Dewey*. Edited by JoAnn Boydston (Carbondale, IL.: Southern Illinois University Press, 1972), vol. 5, pp. 106–109.

[6] George Herbert Mead, *Mind, Self, and Society*. Edited with introduction by Charles W. Morris (Chicago: University of Chicago Press, 1962 [First published in 1934]), pp. 17–18, 77, 140, 260.

[7] *Ibid.*, pp. 78, 82.

[8] *Ibid.*, pp. 90, 154.

[9] *Ibid.*, pp. 171, 265.

[10] *Ibid.*, p. 112.

[11] *Ibid.*, pp. 69, 108–109, 192, 235.

[12] See Mead's treatment of social reconstruction at *ibid.*, pp. 307–310. At other

Without being a direct part of social activism, Mead, in close association with the prestigious Chicago School of sociology, helped to create a new, more consciously manipulative view of the position of social norms in contrast to the passive orientation encouraged by previous cultural paradigms.[13] As these ideas began to spread through society, the more sophisticated interests rather quickly grasped that they could increase their political appeal dramatically by deliberate cultivation of values that enhanced their social status. More recently, these efforts have moved beyond the informal social sphere to the invocation of government itself to aid in the conscious manipulation of individual attitudes. The Labor Department's issuance of regulations requiring that all job titles be phrased in gender neutral terms provides but one example of the influence that this kind of approach had within the Carter Administration.[14]

In American sociology today, Mead's thought, although of major importance, is only one of a variety of ways of looking at society, but fundamentally it shares with much of current sociology a rationale for value relativism that has been too valuable politically to be ignored by interests in search of social legitimation. On this latter point, the sociological attention given to deviance in society has encouraged aspirations to acceptability by interests holding quite a wide range of beliefs. At the same time, the conceptual contributions of sociology to understanding how social values may be refashioned have been of assistance in enhancing the positions of those interests that have been the victims of extra-legal and illegal discrimination. In this regard, one of the best examples in recent times of an interest using legal, political, and social means to reconstruct its position in society is provided by the Black Movement.

The Black Movement: Paradigm for Pluralistic Political Power

In their integration of the techniques of organization, judicial action, direct action, and enhancement of group consciousness, blacks in the twentieth century provide an excellent example of the deliberate movement in essentially peaceful fashion of an outcast group into the main-

---

points Mead's discussion of the importance of community and custom indicates that his thought has some conservative potential. See *ibid.*, pp. 199, 266–267, 273, 320–321.

[13] Mead and sociology are used here as indicators of the normative relativism inherent in much contemporary social science. For example, anthropologists such as Franz Boas and Margaret Mead also helped to contribute to public sympathy toward the relativity of cultural values. Additionally, Mead herself has been seen as an important influence on several areas of psychology. See Merle Curti, *Human Nature in American Thought* (Madison, WI.: University of Wisconsin Press, 1980), pp. 269–270, 347, 359.

[14] See Julia Malone, "Taking Aim at Sexism Lurking Behind Words," *The Christian Science Monitor* (July 8, 1980), p. 19.

stream of the political system. These techniques have been utilized by others as well, but the success of the blacks over several decades in gaining political legitimacy has made their movement a model for interests wishing to influence the political process. The moral worth of the black cause is indisputable, and certainly that fact aided their political efforts. But no matter how praiseworthy an interest's position, that in itself, in the American political process counts for very little. Blacks asserted their claims through effective manipulation of the political system and social norms, and, viewed purely as technique, the methods used must be seen as essentially value neutral. Thus, the approaches used by blacks have been easily adaptable to the efforts of interests with far less worthy aims.

Practically, the first important development in the Black Movement in the twentieth century was the organization of the National Association for the Advancement of Colored People (NAACP) in 1910.[15] The NAACP gave blacks a means for focusing their efforts, for raising funds, for communicating concern about the plight of the Negro, and for linking with sympathetic white leaders. Other black organizations appeared in the decades after 1910, but, during the first half of the century, the NAACP played an important leadership role, primarily because its members had a good sense of how to maneuver effectively within the American political system.

From very early in its existence, the NAACP moved to utilize the courts to protect blacks from injustice and to further policy goals.[16] Their leaders understood that for interests without political legitimacy, such as American blacks, the courts provided the one point of access to the policy process where their claims could at least receive a hearing. Furthermore, through the careful selection of "test cases," cases where the facts were especially favorable to their position, the NAACP was able to obtain Supreme Court support in many instances.[17] Thus, the NAACP was able to use the Supreme Court to obtain important changes in the law of the land, despite the refusal of elected officials to respond constructively to the grievances of blacks. The effects of many of these

---

[15] John Hope Franklin, *From Slavery to Freedom* (Third edition; New York: Vintage Books, 1969), pp. 446–447. Franklin lists John Dewey as one of the participants in the inceptional organizing meeting for the NAACP.

[16] *Ibid.*, p. 447.

[17] See Henry J. Abraham, *The Judicial Process* (Third edition; New York: Oxford University Press, 1975), pp. 233–234. Because experience indicates that generally the Supreme Court is reluctant to decide an issue broader than required by the case before it, the good test case will so intimately interwine the facts and the general issue at stake that the Court will not be able to deal with the former without settling the latter.

Court decisions were enhanced by the NAACP's use of the class action suit, which allowed them to sue on behalf of all blacks disadvantaged by a particular law or practice.[18] Under this approach, a single favorable Court decision became immediately applicable to all blacks suffering the same discrimination as that challenged by the plaintiffs to the case. Moreover, because they were now organized, blacks were able to institute law suits at the local levels to insure that governments throughout the land complied with the law as enunciated by the Supreme Court.

The phase of the Black Movement emphasizing organizational use of the courts reached its climax with the *Brown v. Board of Education* decision. In retrospect, the Brown decision represented the beginning of the end for all legally based racial discrimination in this country. In response to the increasingly supportive judicial climate, blacks intensified their attacks on racial discrimination through greater use of the technique of direct action.[19] Use of this technique was further stimulated by the political success of the 1955–1956 Montgomery, Alabama, bus boycott and the greater involvement of Martin Luther King, Jr., in the movement. The growing militance of blacks culminated with the huge, but peaceful, march on Washington, D.C., in August of 1963. By this point, blacks had aroused considerable sympathy in the country for their demands, a fact which John F. Kennedy had recognized during his presidential campaign with his efforts to have King released from a southern jail. The feeling that something more tangible had to be done in support of what were now seen as legitimate black concerns led to the passage, in 1964, of the first really substantial civil rights legislation in nearly a century. This legislation was followed by the 1965 Voting Rights Act, which at last moved blacks into the political process in significant numbers.

As the Black Movement gained in power and saliency in the 1960s and 1970s, blacks gave more attention to improving their social image, for they recognized that the long-term effectiveness of their political gains

---

[18] Clement E. Vose, "Litigation as a Form of Pressure Group Activity," *Annals of the American Academy of Political and Social Science*, CXXXIX (September, 1958), 24 discusses the advantages of the class action suit. The class action suit is provided for in Rule 23(a) of the Federal Rules of Civil Procedure.

[19] Direct action is also often termed "confrontation politics." It involves the participation of individuals in marches, sit-ins, and other sorts of behavior where those aggrieved act on a mass basis to demonstrate personally their dissatisfaction. See Frances Fox Piven and Richard A. Cloward, *Poor People's Movements* (New York: Vintage Books, 1979), pp. 221–255. Charles E. Silberman, *Crisis in Black and White* (New York: Random House, 1964), pp. 327, 334–335 discusses Saul Alinsky's use of this approach. Stokely Carmichael and Charles V. Hamilton, *Black Power* (New York: Vintage Books, 1967), pp. 132–134 are critical of direct action efforts in the economic area that did not aim for political power.

rested ultimately on their becoming an accepted part of American life and thought. These efforts to establish a sense of black identity and pride gave considerable attention to the role that the American language played in perpetuating an inequitable social structure. Blacks insisted that American language usage be changed to remove the stereotypical racial images that it conveyed.[20] Paralleling these developments was a proliferation of books detailing black contributions to American culture. In many respects, Malcolm X's *Autobiography* and Alex Haley's *Roots* represented the high point of this genre of literature. By the mid-sixties, also, courses in American history and culture in the public schools often contained mandatory segments dealing with the black experience.[21]

The combination of methods used by blacks in conjunction with the obvious moral appeal of their claims, in light of the specific constitutional rights that were denied to them, enabled them to move from a position of exclusion from the political process to one of recognized legitimacy. To be sure, many of their approaches had been used by others. Labor, for example, used direct action widely in the 1930s, and the Jehovah's Witnesses were also highly successful in their pursuit of test cases in the courts. But the Black Movement remains particularly important because it demonstrated that, through skillful manipulation of the diffuse components of the American political process, an interest can not only obtain political influence but can invoke this influence to maneuver government into implementing noneconomic value positions favorable to its members. Although it would not have been possible without the other methods of the movement, the reworking of American values represents the most sophisticated and powerful political technique of the Black Movement.

Governmental Reconstruction of Social Values

The Johnson Administration drew important lessons from the Black Movement, and, in its efforts to build the "Great Society," tried to use governmental powers to construct a social foundation for its policies. Dewey's conception of government as a public-interest grouping reflecting the needs of private groups was no longer sufficiently comprehensive to support the degree of government activism that LBJ envisioned. Liberal egalitarian assumptions were now modified to include the position that, instead of simply responding to the demands made on it, government must create demands on itself essentially by informing the disad-

---

[20] For examples of statements of the need for blacks to redefine themselves, see Malcolm X, *The Autobiography of Malcolm X*. With the assistance of Alex Haley (New York: Ballantine Books, 1965), pp. 162–163, 180–190; Carmichael and Hamilton, *op. cit.*, pp. 35–39.

[21] See Frances Fitzgerald, *America Revised* (Boston: Little, Brown, 1979), pp. [1–2], 97–100.

vantaged of their needs and organizing them to articulate these needs. Thus, a clear aim of Great Society bureaucracies was to build political power groups among the disadvantaged, who would in turn compete with established interests for the attention and largesse of government.[22] But the Great Society's efforts at managed politics produced social ramifications far beyond the articulation of economic needs, for, in attempting to reconstruct the social structure, it necessarily subsidized and encouraged a broad range of values possessed by the newly organized interests.[23] Additionally, interests outside the Johnson Administration's immediate attention span recognized that they, too, with the proper adroitness, could co-opt governmental power on their behalf, with the consequence that government has now become a target for many interests intent on propagating non-economic norms. Indeed, it is seen by some as an important weapon in their struggles to eliminate sin and sell salvation.

American government has, of course, often been invoked on behalf of those waging war on immorality. Most of the earlier efforts, however, aimed simply at the prohibition of that activity regarded as evil. Today, government is being called upon to act in quite a different manner, for many recent appeals to it are asking for its support in redefining the status of beliefs and behavior in order to render them acceptable. Buoyed by the sympathy of many intellectuals toward deviance and their suggestions as to how values may be refashioned, interests are increasingly looking to government to aid them in their endeavors of moral reconstruction. Thus, the focus in the area of criminal activity becomes not the need for punishment, or even for rehabilitation, but the conditions in society that "cause" such behavior. Liberals, unwilling to accept the possibility that human nature itself may contain evil, turn instead to blaming society for crime and violence, and, in doing so, have wreaked all sorts of confusion in the judicial process and the public's mind. By the same token, the standard of consenting adults has been trumpeted as the criterion justifying the widest range of sexual behavior, including incest.[24] And last, but not least, pedophiles find themselves able to claim

---

[22] See John C. Donovan, *The Politics of Poverty* (New York: Pegasus, 1967), p. 43; Frances Fox Piven and Richard A. Cloward, *Regulating the Poor* (New York: Vintage Books, 1972), pp. 266–274; Daniel P. Moynihan, *Maximum Feasible Misunderstanding* (New York: Free Press, 1970), pp. xxiv-xxviii, 97–100.

[23] Some have argued that government intervention on a broad scale into the lives of the poor has fostered and indeed subsidized values antithetical to those necessary to enable the poor to obtain economic security on their own. See George Gilder, *Wealth and Poverty* (New York: Basic Books, 1981).

[24] See "Attacking the Last Taboo," *Time* (April 14, 1980), p. 72. *Time* cites academics from reputable schools who have asserted that consensual incest between adults and children "can sometimes be beneficial." Larry Constantine of the

that children should have the "right" to control their own bodies.[25] No one is suggesting that the contemporary American political system is prepared to move to support *in toto* these interests, but, given the lack of conceptual definition for the basis of governmental authority, it would be foolish at this time to declare out of hand that their claims will remain outside the cloak of government protection.

Even without an administration as deliberately manipulative as that of Lyndon Johnson, interests would have moved to imitate the model provided by the Black Movement. Anyone who is reasonably sensitive to the contemporary social scene can point to numerous interests that see themselves as disadvantaged and that have tried to follow the path pioneered by blacks. Such interests would include women, various ethnic groups, the poor, the handicapped, the aged, and homosexuals. All of these interests have organized, have appealed to the courts, have tried to develop a higher level of identity and consciousness, and have used direct action techniques. In most of these instances, as well, the assault on the political process has been accompanied by the now familiar spate of historical books of decidedly revisionist cast[26] and by claims on particular kinds of usage in the American language. Given the refusal of the reform liberals to deal in the coinage of substantive values, government has been left without standards of social and political acceptability and has been reduced to reacting in a procedural fashion to the claims made on it. In this situation, there are, of course, no foreseeable limits on what in the future might be enunciated as the politically powerful social norms of the day.

Just as the era of economic laissez faire ideology gave way to an era of conscious governmental intervention in the economy, so the current social tolerance of a wide variety of beliefs and practices seems to be moving toward an acceptance of the importance of governmental social intervention and reconstruction. This latter trend threatens the very tolerance and freedom that the reform liberals considered to be important, for their failure to provide a measure of theoretical support for authoritative government *qua* government has left government without the ability to set meaningful limits on social diversity. On the one hand, government institutions are in danger of becoming hopelessly embroiled in the fundamental divisions pulling against social cohesion instead of being able to act to restrain and smooth over such divisions. On the other, acceptance of the optimistic, egalitarian assumptions of modern

---

children's rights movement has gone even further, declaring that children have a "right" to express themselves sexually.

[25] See "Cradle-to-Grave Intimacy," *Time* (September 7, 1981), p. 69.

[26] See generally Fitzgerald's treatment of the effects of this revisionism on America's history texts at the secondary and elementary levels. Fitzgerald, *op. cit.*

liberalism has opened the political process to the serious entreaties of interests that, in former times, would have been considered bizarre, if not outright absurd.

There exists some evidence that, at the level of fundamental personal belief, Americans hold significantly divergent and often irreconcilable positions.[27] Americans have avoided the threats posed to the social fabric by these differences by removing them from their daily interactions with each other. At the political level, the focus on dividing up the economic largesse of the nation has also enabled the diverse interests to interact relatively harmoniously. However, as government moves from simple economic questions to dealing with moral issues, this harmony rapidly dissipates, and the social fabric itself may be threatened. Weak pluralistic government has proven to be increasingly attractive to zealots eager to impose their values on everyone. Sometimes, these values have carried a strongly religious flavor; at other times, the emotion generated by their adherents has radiated all of the intensity of a religious cause. There is little in the background of such interests to suggest to them the value of compromise or the importance of amicable interaction. Indeed, as illustrated by the tactics of those opposing abortion, a wide range of policy issues at the national level can become intertwined with the principled position advocated by a particular interest.[28] Such developments do not point toward the climate of reasoned political debate envisioned by that prophet of instrumentalist democracy, John Dewey, but indicate instead that those institutional and informal sources of social stability that had undergirded weak government are no longer operative.

As Americans have watched their fundamental personal beliefs being fought over in the political arena, they have also been treated to political agitation over claims that many would consider peculiar, if not trivial. Much of the debate over sexual habits and preferences falls into this category. Americans might generally agree, for example, that it is unfair to discriminate against an individual because of his or her sexual preferences, assuming, of course, that they focus on adult human beings. But it is difficult to believe that most Americans think that governmental

---

[27] See Samuel A. Stouffer, *Communism, Conformity, and Civil Liberties* (New York: Doubleday, 1955), pp. 26–57. A recent research effort has supported Stouffer's earlier findings of intolerance among the American public. See John L. Sullivan, James Piereson, George E. Marcus, "An Alternative Conceptualization of Political Tolerance: Illusory Increases 1950s-1970s," *American Political Science Review*, LXXIII (September, 1979), 781–794.

[28] At one point during the latter part of 1979, abortion opponents succeeded in delaying all appropriations for the Labor and Health, Education, and Welfare Departments by attaching anti-abortion amendments to the spending bills for these agencies.

power should be invoked to support and propagate non–heterosexual values, a position which some of the homosexual groups advocate.[29] Of perhaps a more trivial nature are the claims of the animal lovers in America. While few would object to efforts to prevent willful physical cruelty to animals, the more militant animal welfare groups have now moved onto the farms of America to enforce what they see as an animal's rights. *The Wall Street Journal* reports that these groups are prepared to push for "federal legislation outlawing what they call cruel, stressful violations of animals' 'inherent rights.'"[30] These rights go considerably beyond physical mistreatment to what the spokesmen for animal rights see as stressful conditions for animals. They speak in terms of a hog's need to wallow, and a spokesman for the Farm Animal Task Force Action for Life has declared that "non-human animals have certain inalienable rights" including "the right to associate with other animals of their species."[31] As is the case with other groups working to reconstruct society's values, the animal rightists are preparing also to move into the public schools. One suggested program, which so far has been rejected by the schools, would have included questions asking the little tykes what animal they had eaten that day.[32] The emotional power of the animal rightists seems to be considerable, and farm groups, recognizing the vulnerability of the political process to emotional appeals, are taking their efforts seriously. The more significant issue for the entire nation, however, is the effect on important rights and issues of political debate on whether chickens have rights. The trivialization of political debate in the cause of narrow, emotional, and irrational interests is, in essence, the trivialization of human rights in America.

One of the constants, perhaps the constant, throughout the development of Anglo-American liberalism has been the liberals' reliance on the objectivity of science and on its relevance for explanations of the social and political processes. The early liberals professed to be drawing on Newton's ideas in their attempts to justify their theoretical positions. Later, it was Darwin's ideas that were to be particularly important to American liberal thinkers. The reform liberals, who denied metaphysical standards and spoke in terms of process, accepted, without question, that the physical sciences embodied an important form of objective

---

[29] CBS Reports, "Gay Power, Gay Politics" broadcast 10 p.m. EST on Saturday, April 26, 1980, documented the political power of homosexuals in San Francisco and their goal to have their values taught as part of the public school curriculum in that area.

[30] Lynda Schuster, "Livestock Lib," *The Wall Street Journal* (December 18, 1981), p. 1.

[31] Alex Hershaft, "Letters to the Editor," *The Wall Street Journal* (December 30, 1982), p. 7.

[32] Schuster, *op. cit.*, p. 18.

truth, and it was this assumption that led to their infatuation with the application of scientific method to ways of thinking about social relationships. Today, however, the political pluralism and value relativism espoused by the reform liberals have encouraged the politicization of the sciences as well as most other areas of human endeavor. Interests competing for power and legitimacy in the public mind have seen that scientific findings can be a powerful asset in this struggle. Thus, in the past two decades, scientists have often found their views serving as political footballs on the field of politics. Many times, the limitations and validity of their findings are seen as far less important than the ideological purposes that they can be made to serve.

Unfortunately, those using scientific claims to manipulate the public mind for partisan purposes seem to be relying increasingly on what have to be characterized as fear tactics. The public is pelted with assertions that this or that food causes cancer, that cancer will increase because the ozone layer is disappearing, that the disappearance of some minute, hitherto unnoticed, species of life will lead to ecological disaster, or that the gonads of anyone within a particular radius of a nuclear waste site or nuclear plant are in serious danger. In many of the instances involving the partisan use of science, the scientific validity of the public policy positions is at best tenuous, and, in some, it degenerates into blatant emotionalism. The political effects of such emotionalism can be substantial. In the Love Canal incident in Niagara Falls, New York, involving a residential area near a former chemical dumping site, a small group was able to raise enough emotion, despite the lack of any valid scientific evidence of harmful effects from the dump site,[33] to force the state and Federal governments to purchase the homes in the area. Illustrative of the tactics of this effort to invoke the perils of technology in the cause of politics are the remarks by one of its leaders, Lois Gibbs. Ms. Gibbs was reported by her hometown newspaper, the *Buffalo Evening News*, as telling a group in Norton, Ohio, that "they should stop trying to make their point technically and should act like children." The *News*

---

[33] On the lack of valid scientific data, see Robert C. Cowen, "Polluted Science at Love Canal," *The Christian Science Monitor* (June 25, 1980), p. 16; William R. Havender, "The Abuse of Science in Public Policy," *Journal of Contemporary Studies*, IV (Summer, 1981), 9–10. The EPA study released July 14, 1982, found levels of toxicity in houses contiguous to the canal dump site above acceptable levels and declared dwellings in the rest of the area habitable. Lois Gibbs vowed to prevent resettlement in any of the vacated homes in the area despite the facts that most of them had been found habitable and that those who had remained there seem satisfied with the EPA findings. Dan MacDonald, "EPA Conclusions Producing Uncertainty Among Officials," *Buffalo Evening News*, July 15, 1982, p. A-8; Dave Ernst, "Carey Backs Love Canal Study—Says Gibbs Is 'Out of Order,'" *ibid.*, July 23, 1982, p. A-5.

added, "No tactic is too low if you believe in your cause, she says. Fear and hysteria are good weapons."[34]

The ideological power of scientific claims has also manifested itself in the debate over the proper boundaries between church and state. Thus, the "creationists" have challenged the refusal of the public schools to allow their point of view to be presented. The Arkansas trial on this issue involved the use of science by each side of the issue, and, although the creationists lost this effort, there is every indication that they will continue the struggle. They recognize that if they can convince the courts that science adds support to their position, they will then have succeeded in enlisting what is still seen as the final arbiter of issues among Americans and may under this scientific guise be able to move their religious values into the classrooms.

The most unfortunate consequence of this politicization of science is that it has weakened and will continue to weaken both government and science. The reform liberals strongly believed in the compatibility of democratic processes and scientific truth. But now the political processes that they saw as liberating have been used to loosen the moorings of science, the one force in which they ultimately placed their faith. Buffeted by political currents of emotionalism and even hysteria, government agencies have often found themselves more concerned with the political effects of scientific findings than with the need to act on the basis of the findings themselves. Such a stance has a tendency to inhibit scientific research itself, and, of course, the claims made by ideologues in the name of science eventually weaken, in the public mind, the status of science. Attacking the government's inability to distinguish between the constructive and the ideological use of science, William Havender has touched directly on this point by noting the "fostering of a general loss of respect, an erosion of the automatic presumption that science has a special place as an arbiter of truth, which must result from the many unvalidated speculations, gaffes, mistakes, and downright silly claims made in its name...."[35] Science may not provide final answers to questions about the human condition, but it clearly remains an exceptionally important force for material betterment and physical health. The tragic potential in the current political situation is that important scientific warnings of hazards and dangers will be shunted aside in the heat of the group struggle, and that government will be left unable to act with sufficient scientific sophistication and political confidence to respond constructively to such warnings.

---

[34] "Lois Gibbs Has Helpful Hints for Dirty Fight," *Buffalo Evening News* (March 17, 1982), p. A-3.

[35] Havender, *op. cit.*, pp. 15–16.

The Courts: Value Stability under Siege

The courts of England during the eighteenth century and those in the United States in the succeeding centuries played important roles in serving as reference points for social and political values. Wherever they have appeared in this discussion of Anglo-American liberalism, the courts have been seen as forces for social control, and, as the theater of competing interests has become larger, the American courts have survived as the one governmental institution still capable of relatively definitive action. Nevertheless, given the pervasiveness of reform liberal ideology, the inroads of interest-group relativism must of necessity reach toward this bastion of stability as well.

The outlines of modern constitutional doctrine stem from the Supreme Court's 1937 retreat in the face of FDR's threat to "pack" its membership with liberal justices by enlarging it. Since that time, the Court has generally refused to uphold challenges to the constitutionality of economic legislation and has used its power of judicial review primarily in cases involving individual rights and liberties. The Court had considered cases of the latter sort prior to 1937, but, after that date, it developed what has been perceptively termed a "guardian ethic"[36] towards those perceived to be among the disadvantaged in American society. This stance was encouraged by the increasing frequency with which organizations turned to the courts for remedies for social wrongs and by the pressures that these interests brought to bear on presidential selection of judges.[37] The forces favoring judicial social activism achieved their greatest successes under the Warren Court, which quite literally undertook a judicially sponsored reconstruction of American society in a manner that threatened to inundate the courts with the kind of interest-group conflict that characterized the more obviously political branches of government.

Before an interest can hope to obtain a favorable court decision, it must first have standing to sue. This standing-to-sue requirement serves as a barrier to frivolous and non-legal claims or complaints and has over the years prevented many of the more esoteric interests from gaining access to the courts. Karen Orren, in an important study of interest activity in the courts, has shown that the Warren Court and early Burger Court acted to liberalize considerably the requirements for standing to sue in the Federal courts. She is clear that this is of a piece with interest activity throughout the political process.

---

[36] Ward E. Y. Elliott, *The Rise of Guardian Democracy* (Cambridge, MA.: Harvard University Press, 1974).

[37] President Carter responded to these pressures by appointing more women, blacks, and chicanos to the Federal courts than any previous president. Almost all were, of course, Democrats. See Sheldon Goldman, "A Profile of Carter's Judicial Nominees," *Judicature*, LXII (November, 1978), 247–254.

...In the course of a spring tide of group activity in society generally, the liberalized approach has enabled numerous environmental, consumer, historical-preservational, and other associations, as well as a variety of ad hoc citizens' groups, to come before the court to do battle.... The bid of these organizations for standing is a continuation of energetic efforts in Congress, the administrative agencies, and the judicial process itself....[38]

Obviously, the widening of the threshold requirement for standing to sue presents an opportunity for increased interest pressure on the supreme law of the land as formulated by the Supreme Court.

Attempts of interests to involve government in the construction and propagation of a wide variety of personal, intangible values have found a parallel in the Court's willingness to open the standing-to-sue requirement to include intangible values not previously given legal status. Orren shows that the Court has consciously moved away from limiting standing to sue to those who could show tangible injury to a right protected by statute or by the Constitution. For example, interests that have charged that governmental action will damage their aesthetic enjoyment of the environment have convinced the Court that such injury is sufficient to allow them standing to sue. This approach, in Orren's words, reached the point of "trivialization" of the standing test in the SCRAP case.[39]

In this case, five law students who had organized as Students Challenging Regulatory Agency Procedures joined with other environmental organizations to enjoin a rate increase that the Interstate Commerce Commission had granted the railroads. The plaintiffs argued that the increase should not be allowed without the filing of an environmental impact statement. SCRAP claimed standing to sue on the grounds that the five students were hikers, sightseers, and other forms of recreational users of the natural areas in and around the D.C. metropolitan area and that, among other points, the rate surcharge would cause them aesthetic and other harm by increasing the amount of litter due to the higher cost of transporting recyclable materials. The plaintiffs eventually lost their case, but the important point here is that the Court allowed SCRAP standing to sue based on its highly attenuated, and what the non-lawyer of merely average intelligence must regard simply as absurd, claims of injury. Justice Stewart, speaking for the Court, declared:

...Aesthetic and environmental well-being, like economic well-being, are important ingredients of the quality of life in our society, and the fact that particular environmental interests are shared by the many rather than the few does not make them less deserving of legal protection through the judicial process....[40]

---

[38] Karen Orren, "Standing to Sue: Interest Group Conflict in the Federal Courts," *American Political Science Review*, LXX (September, 1976), 735.

[39] *Ibid.*, p. 738.

[40] *U.S.* v. *SCRAP* 412 US 669 (1973), at 686 citing *Sierra Club* v. *Morton* 405 US 727 (1972), at 734.

Speaking for himself, Chief Justice Burger, and Justice Rehnquist in dissent on the issue of standing to sue, Justice White termed the claims of SCRAP "so remote, speculative and insubstantial in fact that they fail to confer standing...."[41] He added that, if standing were permitted in this case, "we are well on our way to permitting citizens at large to litigate any decisions of the Government which fall in an area of interest to them and with which they disagree."[42]

In the United States, the courts have had as their guide a written Constitution that contains sufficient ambiguity to allow flexible interpretation yet—for one following a literal reading of its words—appears to set standards for the exercise of power. As the Court has moved away from protecting economic rights, a prime concern of the authors of the Constitution, it has been forced to contort and even ignore the words of that document. In recent times, the clearest examples of this sort of approach occurred under the Warren Court.

In the *Bolling* v. *Sharpe*[43] decision, the companion case to *Brown* v. *Board of Education*, the Warren Court first demonstrated its willingness to legislate public policy by elevating social ends over constitutional means. The Brown decision relied on the Equal Protection Clause of the Fourteenth Amendment to rule unconstitutional segregation in the public schools. Unfortunately, there is no equal protection clause that applies to the national government. The Warren Court handled this lack in the Bolling case by simply reading such a meaning into the due process portion of the Fifth Amendment in a manner that was hardly a model for rigorous judicial logic.

> ... But the concepts of equal protection and due process, both stemming from our American ideal of fairness, are not mutually exclusive. The "equal protection of the laws" is a more explicit safeguard of prohibited unfairness than "due process of law," and, therefore, we do not imply that the two are always interchangeable phrases....[44]

The real problem for the Court, one which it could not answer with logic, was posed by the existence of a due process clause in the Fourteenth Amendment that applied to the states. Yet the Court refused even to consider its applicability to the question of racial school segregation by the states,[45] making the act of judicial legislation in the Bolling decision even more blatant. One can not fault the goals achieved by the Court in the area of racial segregation, but the cavalier means used provide a poor precedent for later courts bent on imposing their, perhaps less worthy, values on the country.

---

[41] *Ibid.*, at 723.
[42] *Ibid.*
[43] 347 US 497 (1954).
[44] *Ibid.*, at 499.
[45] *Brown* v. *Board of Education* 347 US 483 (1954), at 495.

The Warren Court again exercised its penchant for judicial legislating in particularly egregious fashion in its consideration of a Connecticut statute prohibiting the use of contraceptives.[46] The justices had obviously made up their minds that the statute was unwise, but they were without a specific constitutional clause protecting an individual's privacy in such a matter. Speaking for the Court, Justice Douglas delivered his "penumbra" interpretation of the Bill of Rights as applied to the states through the Fourteenth Amendment. There was, stated Douglas, no specific constitutional protection of marital privacy, but "specific guarantees in the Bill of Rights have penumbras, formed by emanations from those guarantees that help give them life and substance. . . ."[47] These "emanations," in Douglas's opinion, encompassed a right to marital privacy, which the justice, who was to be thrice-divorced and four times married expounded upon with the observation that "[m]arriage is a coming together for better or worse, hopefully enduring, and intimate to the degree of being sacred. . . ."[48] To the Court's credit, the majority did not follow the path suggested by three of the justices, which would have been to use the rights retained by the people phrase in the Ninth Amendment, an approach that would have established a constitutional precedent of essentially boundless subjectivity. Still, the Court took it upon itself in this case to legislate, or create, a right that nowhere existed in the Constitution.

Only Justices Black and Stewart seemed capable of sufficient perspective to see the subjective, relativistic ramifications of the Court's position in the Griswold case. Typically, Justice Black went right to the point with his statement that "I like my privacy as well as the next one, but I am nevertheless compelled to admit that government has a right to invade it unless prohibited by some specific constitutional provision. . . ."[49] Justice Stewart, joining Justice Black in dissent, also found serious problems with holding the Connecticut statute, "an uncommonly silly law," unconstitutional without a clear constitutional basis for doing so.[50]

Griswold and Bolling stand at the apex of subjective judicial legislation by the Warren Court, which did not hesitate to play fast and loose with a number of constitutional clauses.[51] The importance of the two cases stems from their demonstration of the Court's willingness to move

---

[46] The case was *Griswold v. Connecticut* 381 US 479 (1965).
[47] *Ibid.*, at 484.
[48] *Ibid.*, at 486.
[49] *Ibid.*, at 510.
[50] *Ibid.*, at 527–531.
[51] For a discussion of other examples of the Court's legislative demeanor, see Christopher Wolfe, "A Theory of U.S. Constitutional History," *The Journal of Politics*, XCIII (May, 1981), 304–308; Macklin Fleming, *The Price of Perfect Justice* (New York: Basic Books, 1974), pp. 89–98, 114–120.

completely away from the wording of the Constitution in pursuit of ends that the justices deemed worthy. Furthermore, each of the cases illustrates the increased concern of the Court in enforcing moral values, although the force of the Equal Protection Clause does lie behind the Bolling decision. On the other hand, the Griswold decision deals directly with questions of personal morality and stands as an uneasy precedent for claims of constitutional protection for all sorts of private conduct.

In light of the Court's readiness to respond positively to interests claiming rights without any specific legislative or constitutional basis, it is not surprising that some scholars have argued that the Court no longer sees itself as an interpreter of the Constitution but as a legislator. One of these arguments sees "social welfare" as determined by the justices, not as found in the wording of the Constitution, as the predominating factor in Supreme Court decisions.[52] Others have not been hesitant to suggest problems in the legislative stance of the justices, pointing out that there is a real question whether judges are capable of resolving social welfare issues in the constructive, flexible manner that such questions often require. As early as 1825, in a famous dissenting opinion to the majority's exercise of judicial review in a Pennsylvania Supreme Court case,[53] Judge Gibson argued that the legislature, with its openness to political and social considerations, was far better equipped to determine social policy than the courts, which were limited to the formalized channels of the judicial process. More recently, Donald Horowitz has also raised serious questions about the capacity of the courts to act as formulators of the general welfare. Focusing on the courts themselves in the judicial process, Horowitz argues persuasively that judges are essentially limited to responding to the pleas of particular litigants, that cases are often examples of the worst kinds of misconduct, that judges tend to limit themselves to the information presented to them on an issue, and that they have no effective means of following up on the implementation of their decisions.[54] Finally, Orren points out that today the Supreme Court's dependence on the formalities of the judicial process has led the Court to assume that organizations before it do, in fact, represent the feelings of the broad interests for whom they claim to speak, even when there may be little evidence that such is the case.[55] This has rendered its

---

[52] Wolfe, op. cit., p. 307. The criticism of Wolfe by Lief H. Carter, "Think Things Not Words," The Journal of Politics, XCIII (May, 1981), 315–321, is an excellent example of the confusion that the judicial relativists exhibit as they move away from the words of the Constitution.

[53] Eakin v. Raub, 12 Sergeant & Rawles 330, Pennsylvania Reports (1825).

[54] Donald Horowitz, The Courts and Social Policy (Washington, D.C.: Brookings Institution, 1977), pp. 25–62, 255–274.

[55] Orren, op. cit., pp. 735–741.

view of social reality subject to exploitation by the maneuvers of organized interests. In sum, courts simply lack the kind of political knowledge and openness to compromise that is essential to working through social problems. These shortcomings are a serious liability when the Supreme Court tries to work within the broad generalities that are often contained in congressional statutes. They have every prospect of being fatal to the status of judicial power if the Court allows itself to be enticed into legislating normative values for society.

The policy position of the courts is important to the overall question of the effects of Anglo-American liberal thought on governmental authority because the courts are one of the last governmental institutions capable of rising above the scramble of organized interests. For a time, in response to attacks from the reform liberals, the Supreme Court removed itself from the policy area by deferring to legislative judgments on economic issues. But the long-run goal of reform liberalism was to enlist the courts in support of social reform, and certainly the Warren Court responded very favorably to this goal. However, as Herbert Croly pointed out long ago, social reform is a term without substance or normative definition. Liberalism's answer to this problem has been to turn the political process over to competing interests with the assumption that whatever balance is achieved reflects the social good. These interests have moved beyond drawing economic rewards from government to utilizing government itself for the propagation and enforcement of normative values. In these efforts, the courts remain important prizes to be brought under the process relativism of the reform liberal ideology because they can play a significant role in defining and establishing social norms.

In many respects, the political achievements of the homosexual community can provide a gauge as to how far government can be manipulated on behalf of those wishing to change social values. Already, the homosexuals have successfully used many of the techniques employed by the Black Movement, and they are a political power of importance in San Francisco and other major cities.[56] Yet the courts generally remain an important barrier to the politically approved imposition of homosexual values on society. If the courts do grant legal status to these values one can expect a fundamental refashioning of American mores. Naturally, other interests outside the bounds of common social acceptability are watching the Gay Movement closely. Given the growing sophistication of interests in manipulating social attitudes and the inability of reform liberalism to provide government with a functional rationale for substan-

---

56 See "New Power Bloc: Urban Homosexuals," *U.S. News and World Report* (June 4, 1979), p. 13.

tive normative standards, one would have to conclude that the times favor the eventual success of the advocates of homosexual rights. And it does not require a great deal of foresight or imagination for one to suggest that this achievement will not delimit, or even stabilize for any significant time, the bounds of political legitimacy in America.

Conclusions

A s liberal thought has evolved, the focus on individual freedoms has drawn attention from the debt that these values owe to the stable social contexts in which they have been formulated. Hobbes, who lived much of his life in unsettled times, had no difficulty seeing the importance of social stability for the individual, and he tried to construct a political system that would ensure such a condition. With Locke, liberalism was already assuming social cohesion and concentrating on questions of individual protections. The approaches to social control became significantly more sophisticated in the thought of Bentham and in practice under the apologists for laissez faire. In America, however, the laissez faire ideas that originated in England and their accompanying scientific claims found a markedly different social context. Contrasted with the mother country, America was a society of widely varying interests, and unarticulated forces of social control could not be expected to function long unchallenged.

Darwin's ideas provided American reform liberals with a vehicle for challenging the ideology of limited government, but this approach had serious ramifications for society and government. Value judgments were deliberately left at the mercy of group competition, and government was defined as a part of this competition. Today this process has reached the point where, through the growth of sub-governmental relationships, interests have become an informal, but powerful, part of the governmental system. This development and its underlying ideological perspective have had the effect of immersing government in the maelstrom of social conflict. The expansion of governmental regulation and social intervention reflects the inability of public officials to maintain a position of leadership. Increasingly dependent on interest support, these officials have found themselves political prisoners of the deep differences in society and have been left unable to move firmly against threats to the system and the individuals in it. Made during a recent congressional confrontation over abortion, Senator Lowell Weicker's complaint that "[t]en million people [are] out of work and we're debating each other's values" summarizes remarkably well the plight of government without authoritative identity or substantive conceptual definition.

Most Americans would probably agree that big government does not necessarily lead to effective government. In fact, the larger government has grown and the more extensively it has impinged on people's daily lives, the less capable of coherent, decisive action it has appeared. Hopefully, the foregoing examination of the Anglo-American liberal heritage has shown that the shortcomings of American government are not primarily technical in nature but are due to underlying conceptual difficulties. Democratic government in a society as diverse as that of the United States can not be responsive to a wide range of competing social norms and still be able to act forcefully. Governmental officials must be able to draw on ideological resources that enable them to establish a position sufficiently independent of social interests to allow them to construct a viable definition of the public good and to concentrate on resolving threats to that good. Liberalism has not provided such resources, and it is vitally important that Americans understand why.

During much of the past two centuries, liberals were able to avoid confronting the importance of government for social control because other means of control were effective. These non-governmental forces for social control came to the fore just as liberalism began to accept the idea of limited government and expanded individual economic freedom. Thus the force of self-discipline in the factory and other institutions in liberal society has played an important role in maintaining social stability. The same has been true for the rhetoric of individual enterprise and the harsh facts of economic life. It is not at all clear that liberals were aware that their ideological individualism was undergirded by these forces of control. One of the major problems of the current era is that the corrosive effects of value relativity have weakened these elements of social control, and liberalism has not been able to construct a viable alternative through government.

At the same time that liberal theorists have been derelict in their considerations of the basis for government authority, they have been enthusiastic in their efforts to embrace the ideas of the physical sciences and to apply them to political and social thought. The association of science and social theory has proceeded in an uncritical fashion and today appears to be fraught with danger for individual freedom. Although Newton's ideas contributed to the development of individual liberty by suggesting to economists and others that society operated according to natural laws after the fashion of the universe, it was really Locke's epistemological assumptions that supported liberal individualism. At its base, liberal psychology assumed the existence of an entity called the "mind" which responded to external stimuli and conceived ideas and beliefs. Such a position left each individual a discrete entity, separate and unique from his fellow beings and entitled to political protection for his individualism.

With the advent of Darwin's ideas, the classical liberal conception of mind was seriously weakened, and the underlying rationale for individualism was thereby threatened. Thinkers such as Dewey and Mead postulated a psychology that saw mind not as an entity unto itself but as simply a stage in the flow of social interaction. Human consciousness became essentially a reflection of society's attitudes and beliefs. With this position, the individual became an integrated part of society, incapable of declaring his or her intrinsic independence or worth separate from it. Most recently, Richard Rorty has carried this line of reasoning to the point of rejecting what, over the past several centuries, has been seen as the essential element of the philosophical enterprise. Philosophy, he has asserted, should cast aside its claims to be searching for an epistemologically objective basis for human existence.[1] Contrary to the beliefs of the seventeenth-century and Enlightenment liberal thinkers, there is no inner metaphysical essence possessed by man, and philosophical efforts directed toward defining such an entity are doomed to failure and will only perpetuate confusions about the human condition.[2] All of man's beliefs and actions are physiologically explainable. There are no "ghosts" within the human body.[3]

Obviously the positions of Dewey and Rorty provide exceptionally weak bases for the assertion of individual rights in terms of intrinsic individual worth and uniqueness. Rorty, for example, fails to recognize the importance of political ideology when he states that his position poses minimal danger to individual freedom because the means for personal manipulation already exist.[4] What he does not see is that the liberal political ideology of individual freedom developed from and has been tied to a particular epistemological view of the individual and that his position and those of his relativistic "heroes" in philosophy have now destroyed that basis for liberal ideology.[5] Much of the confusion that surrounds the idea of individual rights can be traced to the current

---

[1] Richard Rorty, *Philosophy and the Mirror of Nature* (Princeton: Princeton University Press, 1980), pp. 315–316, 329 n. 14.

[2] *Ibid.*, pp. 357, 373.

[3] *Ibid.*, pp. 157, 354, 387.

[4] *Ibid.*, p. 354.

[5] Rorty does clearly recognize the importance of science to the western liberal philosophical tradition. See for example *ibid.*, pp. 131, 387. His use of the appellation "heroes" occurs on p. 382.

untenability of the classical liberal epistemology. It is, of course, possible to retain both the more modern, and perhaps more scientific, psychological positions and governmental protection of individual rights. But, to do so, the misconceptions involved in the applications of science and its methodologies to social relations must first be cleared away. Additionally, it would seem to be incumbent on thinkers such as Rorty to acknowledge the serious political effects of their positions, and one would hope that these intellectuals would finally step forward with a forthright statement on the importance of values, a position with which Rorty does seem sympathetic, although he does not develop it.[6]

It seems clear that human freedom is an important, if not essential, condition for the advancement of science. Without the freedom of individuals to challenge ideas and to pursue whatever lines of inquiry they deem important, science is left without its most important impetus. Thus, the liberal infatuation with the application of science to the political realm has in a way reversed the proper relationship. The political protection of individual liberties has aided tremendously in the advancement of science, and, historically, an amenable political and social climate has made modern science possible.

The conclusion to be drawn from a correct understanding of the relationship between science and political ideology and practice is that science and human freedom can each prosper if the sources of political values are derived from something other than attempts to apply science to the political. The values of political society must be recognized to be artificial in the Burkean sense. They are human contrivances that have shown over time that they are valuable in enabling men to live better lives. In this sense, they may be seen as part of the western civilized tradition and as grounded in the needs of real people, not in the ultimately metaphysical claims of scientific inevitability.[7]

Candid recognition of the importance of values and of their artificial nature appears to be a constructive alternative to the relativism proffered by the reform liberals. Dewey's position was that the universe is constantly changing and that, scientifically, the political process must also be open to constant change, a condition that human beings are incapable of sustaining.[8] If the universe is infinite and there are no final answers, then the reform liberals are left with some sort of ideological temporary

---

[6] See *ibid.*, pp. 335–336.

[7] In terms of providing sounder foundations for values, efforts by responsible intellectuals such as Alasdair MacIntyre are of tremendous importance. See Alasdair MacIntyre, *After Virtue* (Notre Dame, IN.: University of Notre Dame Press, 1981).

[8] See Fitzgerald's discussion of the impact on American education of Dewey's denigration of the value of history. Frances Fitzgerald, *America Revised* (Boston: Little, Brown, 1979), pp. 173–175.

housing at any given point in time, and such housing bears all of the disabilities of its hasty construction and transitory nature. Society can not survive free without a government capable of providing direction, and such a government is impossible without an acceptance of fundamental values. But it is the responsibility of the democratic citizen to insist that these values accurately reflect the needs of the human condition. He must be willing to recognize his limitations and inequalities. Simply asserting the equality of everyone and the political parity of all normative claims is ideologically destructive. As contemporary events have shown, this approach may leave government without the authority even to enforce rules for the game of politics.

Surveying the liberal tradition, one is struck by the real dangers created by the failure to articulate fundamental goals and values. The reliance on human reason and on science, useful weapons for forcing change but highly unstable as social foundations, has left liberal thought without stable normative protections for the individual. It is time that the social importance of fundamental values be recognized. Thus, it is necessary for American schools to concern themselves with basic personal values such as honesty, tolerance, courage, initiative, and love of nation.[9] These are not discriminatory values; nor is it easy to see how they might detract from building better citizens. They are, however, substantive values and should be taught as such. As a child matures, he or she can, of course, move on to other more complex normative judgments. But with a basic beginning, the child will at least have a sense of right and wrong and a feeling for the importance and respectability of normative judgments. Such attitudes should be helpful for better citizenship as well.

At the same time, government must refrain from partisan manipulation of substantive social values. It must draw on the strengths of social pluralism, and, to do this, it must distance itself from the give and take that moves the nation toward social consensus on issues. By intervening on behalf of a particular interest, government immediately lessens the flexibility involved in the pluralistic construction of substantive values. In this respect, the First Amendment freedoms of speech and religion are far more important than the Founding Fathers could have envisioned. Today, in a maneuver anticipated by Hobbes, interests have attempted to invoke governmental sanction to impose specific kinds of language usage on the population. They recognize that language patterns beliefs. But in a democratic context, the politicization of language can only lead to

---

[9] For a good discussion of approaches to encouraging recognition of basic values, see George C. S. Benson and Thomas S. Engeman, *Amoral America* (Revised edition; Durham, N.C.: Carolina Academic Press, 1982) generally and with reference to teaching values pp. 97–108, 177–178.

greater social divisiveness and weaker government. American governments must return to the precepts of the First Amendment and support the position that they have no business telling people how they should speak, what they should believe, or how they should pray. Such a stance does not mean that government should use derogatory or discriminatory language. Nor does it leave interests unprotected, for most interests are now clearly capable of protecting themselves. When Jesse Jackson called for a black boycott of a major brewery, that company moved quickly to respond to the issues involved. When homosexuals brought sufficient pressure to bear, the American Psychiatric Association changed the designation of homosexuality from that of pathological condition to that of one in which individual maladjustments may occur. These are but examples of the myriad adjustments occurring privately among social interests. In the long run, these compromises strengthen society and provide government with a base of social agreement from which it can act to deal with those issues that are serious threats to the nation.

Power has determined social advantage in liberal systems just as it has in other political systems, but, with few exceptions, the liberal ideology has left the sources of this power unexamined, thereby exacerbating its arbitrary character. As Lowi and Lippmann have suggested, governmental institutions can assist the citizen in assigning responsibility for the exercise of power. Lippmann's reliance on the executive for policy leadership and implementation has a great deal of merit, but it may be that today's executive has already become severely hampered by its political context. Of more importance appears to be the power of the courts to force both the executive and legislative branches to take responsibility for their decisions and to insist that these branches allow social cohesion to develop naturally.

For government to regain the ability to act firmly and authoritatively, two preliminary steps must be taken. First, government officials must be forced to take responsibility for their decisions. Second, these officials must be given an institutional context in which their decisions can be effectively implemented. Lowi's reliance on the courts is an important suggestion in both respects. The courts remain capable of insisting that legislatures act candidly in their legislative enactments, assuming, of course, that the courts themselves are willing to abide by the words of the Constitution. The exercise of policy should be returned to the legislature, and the courts should prevent legislatures from trying to bury real policy decisions in the depths of the bureaucracy through the passage of ambiguous statutes lacking meaningful standards. To the plea that ambiguity is often necessary in order to obtain a majority in the legislature, the answer might well be made that if a clearly stated position can not obtain a majority, then it does not deserve to become law.

Hiding a legislative policy position behind a smokescreen of empty verbiage merely accentuates the hypocrisy of the political process.

Today the courts retain the capacity to provide intellectual leadership backed with power. By insisting on the proper exercise of governmental power, they can enhance the general level of governmental authority and encourage the natural development of social norms and cohesion. But to remain effective and authoritative American judges must be ever sensitive to the fact that their status derives largely from the limited nature of their function. They are not political representatives of particular interests. Yet presently their positions are tenuously balanced, for they have become targets of those who wish to draw them into the general dynamics of interest group politics, and, in responding to such entreaties, some among the judiciary will undoubtedly be sorely tempted to see themselves as the saviors of society. When, in the past century and a half, the courts have suffered from sustained public criticism, they usually have been guilty of unjustifiable activism. Judges can not be all things to all people; nor can they effectively extend themselves to act as surrogates for other public officials. Judicial behavior is the result of a peculiar kind of educational background and structured official context, and it is the parameters legitimated by these factors that give credence to a judge's activities. Judges are out of their element acting as administrators, school boards, or legislators, and the public is quick to sense this. Thus, attempts to make the legal process more susceptible to the interest-group struggle, if successful, could be highly corrosive to the status of the judiciary. The short-term gains that might be achieved on the behalf of particular interests would be minuscule in comparison to the permanent damage that would be inflicted on governmental authority. In a very real sense, the American people have chosen the courts as the ultimate guardians of the verities of the American political culture, an act that reflects their deep need for some source of authoritative, yet accessible, decisions. Further political incursions on the judicial process will only continue the weakening of governmental authority and increase the unease and frustration of the American people.

Indeed there may be important lessons for other governmental institutions to be gained from the experience of the judiciary. This is particularly true for the bureaucracies of government. Administrative personnel also answer to a sense of professionalism and presumably could work toward increased standards of objectivity in the formulation and implementation of governmental regulations. This, of course, would require renunciation of the informal understandings that have made agencies representatives of particular interests. The Constitution, however, envisions only the President and Congress as the representative bodies of the nation, and it might enhance the status of government if the public were to insist on a return to the intentions of the Founding Fathers. Such an eventuality would necessarily involve a fundamental reorientation in the attitudes and behavior of organized interests in this country.

An additional adjustment that would improve the policy process at the national level would be to make the terms of the members of the House of Representatives coterminous with that of the President. Such a change, relatively minor and simple in itself, would increase tremendously the power of the executive by making his election and that of the House responsive to the same public mood. It would also free congressmen from constant concern about re-election and the pressures of interests involved therein and would further insulate some of them from special interests by allowing them protection under the political aegis of a President from their party. This institutional change along with greater court scrutiny of the procedures of power and authority would contribute a great deal toward making government more effective. Nonetheless, such measures will be only temporary palliatives if American intellectuals continue to refuse to recognize the importance of values contributing to authoritative government in American life. Without an ideology that affirms the importance of powerful government within a democratic context, Americans will most assuredly face the stark prospect of the former without the latter.

In their attachment to process, the reform liberals have highlighted an essential ingredient of effective democratic government. But procedure is just one of the elements of meaningful democratic government. To defer to process as the answer to the difficult issues arising among interests is to invite weak government and ultimately to discredit democracy itself. The American system has not yet reached the point where pitched battles in the streets are common events. But it is no longer uncommon for the zealots on particular issues to take direct physical action that leads to clashes with the authorities. Government must insist that grievances be channeled through proper constitutional forms while making clear that it also is responsible to constitutional democratic procedures. Only in this manner can the public authorities remove the conditions of social and political instability that foster totalitarianism. Strong government will, of course, produce strong consequences for some. But no government can satisfy everyone. The essential point is that only a government that can be effective can command the respect and support that are essential to the continued health of a democratic system.

Despite the precarious condition of much of the world and the conceptual disabilities of America's dominant political ideology, it is far from inevitable that the present era will be seen as the final chapter in the liberal saga. The liberal position clearly possesses sufficient flexibility to incorporate more directive values and yet maintain its appeal to the average American. Whatever its flaws, liberal thought has been the framework for a sustained development of individual freedom and material prosperity unequalled in the history of the world. With the proper tuning, it is still capable of defeating the efforts of the children of darkness and moving the human race to even greater levels of achievement.

Sources Cited

Books

Abbott, Philip, *The Shotgun Behind the Door*. Athens, GA.: University of Georgia Press, 1976.

Abraham, Henry J., *The Judicial Process*. Third edition; New York: Oxford University Press, 1975.

Albee, Ernest, *A History of English Utilitarianism*. New York: Macmillan Company, 1957.

Atiyah, P. S., *The Rise and Fall of Freedom of Contract*. Oxford: Clarendon Press, 1979.

Bannister, Robert C., *Social Darwinism*. Philadelphia: Temple University Press, 1979.

Bell, Daniel, *The End of Ideology*. New, revised edition; New York: Collier Books, 1962.

Benson, George C. S., and Thomas S. Engeman, *Amoral America*. Revised edition; Durham, N.C.: Carolina Academic Press, 1982.

Bentham, Jeremy, *A Fragment on Government* and *An Introduction to the Principles of Morals and Legislation*. Edited with introduction by Wilfrid Harrison. Oxford: Basil Blackwell, 1948.

Bentley, Arthur F., *The Process of Government*. Evanston, IL.: Principia Press, 1949.

Berman, Daniel M., *It Is So Ordered*. New York: W. W. Norton, 1966.

Bernstein, Richard J., *John Dewey*. New York: Washington Square Press, 1966.

Bourne, Randolph, *War and the Intellectuals: Essays, 1915–1919*. Edited with introduction by Carl Resek. New York: Harper and Row, 1964.

Briggs, Asa, *Victorian People*. New York: Harper and Row, 1963.

Brinton, Crane, *English Political Thought in the Nineteenth Century*. Cambridge, MA.: Harvard University Press, 1949.

Broom, Leonard, and Philip Selznick, *Sociology*. Third edition; New York: Harper and Row, 1963.

Buchanan, James M., and Richard E. Wagner, *Democracy in Deficit*. New York: Academic Press, 1977.

Burke, Edmund, *Reflections on the Revolution in France*. Edited with introduction by Thomas H. D. Mahoney. Indianapolis: Bobbs-Merrill, 1955.

Cahill, Fred V., *Judicial Legislation*. New York: The Ronald Press, 1952.

Carmichael, Stokely, and Charles V. Hamilton, *Black Power*. New York: Vintage Books, 1967.

Carpenter, William Seal, *Foundations of Modern Jurisprudence*. New York: Appleton-Century-Crofts, 1958.

Cash, W. F., *The Mind of the South*. New York: Alfred A. Knopf, 1941.

Catlin, George E. G., *The Story of the Political Philosophers*. New York: McGraw-Hill, 1939.

Clive, John, *Macaulay*. New York: Vintage Books, 1975.

Commager, Henry Steele, *The American Mind*. New Haven: Yale University Press, 1950.

Conwell, Russell H., *Acres of Diamonds*. New York: Harper and Row, 1915.

Corwin, Edward S., *American Constitutional History*. Edited by Alpheus T. Mason and Gerald Garvey. New York: Harper and Row, 1964.

Coser, Lewis A., *Masters of Sociological Thought*. New York: Harcourt Brace Jovanovich, 1971.

Cremin, Lawrence A., *The Transformation of the School*. New York: Vintage, 1961.

Croly, Herbert, *The Promise of American Life*. Introduction by Charles Forcey. New York: E. P. Dutton, 1963.

Crozier, Michael J., Samuel P. Huntington, and Joji Watanuki, *The Crisis of Democracy*. New York: New York University Press, 1975.

Curti, Merle, *The Growth of American Thought*. Second edition; New York: Harper and Brothers, 1951.

———, *Human Nature in American Thought*. Madison, WI.: University of Wisconsin Press, 1980.

Danford, John W., *Wittgenstein and Political Philosophy.* Chicago: University of Chicago Press, 1978.

Dewey, John, *A Common Faith.* New Haven: Yale University Press, 1934.

———, *Essays in Experimental Logic.* Chicago: University of Chicago Press, 1916.

———, *The Influence of Darwin on Philosophy and Other Essays in Contemporary Thought.* New York: Henry Holt and Company, 1910.

———, *Liberalism and Social Action.* New York: Capricorn Books, 1963.

———, *The Philosophy of John Dewey.* Edited by John J. McDermott. 2 vols. New York: G. P. Putnam's Sons, 1973.

———, *The Public and Its Problems.* Chicago: Gateway Books, 1946.

Donovan, John C., *The Politics of Poverty.* New York: Pegasus, 1967.

Ducat, Craig R., *Modes of Constitutional Interpretation.* St. Paul, MN.: West Publishing, 1978.

Dunn, John, *Political Obligation in Its Historical Context.* Cambridge: Cambridge University Press, 1980.

Eaton, Clement, *The Freedom-of-Thought Struggle in the Old South.* Revised and enlarged edition; New York: Harper and Row, 1964.

Elliott, Ward E. Y., *The Rise of Guardian Democracy.* Cambridge, MA.: Harvard University Press, 1974.

Everett, Charles Warren, *The Education of Jeremy Bentham.* New York: Columbia University Press, 1931.

Fine, Sidney, *Laissez Faire and the General-Welfare State.* Ann Arbor, MI.: University of Michigan Press, 1969.

Fitzgerald, Frances, *America Revised.* Boston: Little, Brown, 1979.

Fitzhugh, George, *Cannibals All! or Slaves Without Masters.* Cambridge, MA.: Harvard University Press, 1960.

Fleming, Macklin, *The Price of Perfect Justice.* New York: Basic Books, 1974.

Franklin, John Hope, *From Slavery to Freedom.* Third edition; New York: Vintage Books, 1969.

Franklin, Julian H., *John Locke and the Theory of Sovereignty.* Cambridge: Cambridge University Press, 1978.

Foucault, Michel, *Discipline and Punish.* Translated by Alan Sheridan. New York: Pantheon Books, 1977.

———, *Power/Knowledge.* Translated by Colin Gordon, et al. Edited by Colin Gordon. New York: Pantheon Books, 1980.

Gilder, George, *Wealth and Poverty*. New York: Basic Books, 1981.

Goldman, Eric F., *Rendezvous with Destiny*. Revised edition; New York: Alfred A. Knopf, 1956.

Gutmann, Amy, *Liberal Equality*. Cambridge: Cambridge University Press, 1980.

Halevy, Elie, *The Growth of Philosophical Radicalism*. Translated by Mary Morris. Boston: Beacon Press, 1955.

Hay, Douglas, et.al., *Albion's Fatal Tree.* New York: Pantheon Books, 1975.

Heilbroner, Robert, *An Inquiry Into the Human Prospect.* New York: W. W. Norton, 1974.

Hill, Christopher, *The World Turned Upside Down*. New York: Viking Press, 1973.

Himmelfarb, Gertrude, *Victorian Minds*. New York: Alfred A. Knopf, 1968.

Hobbes, Thomas, *Leviathan*. Edited with introduction by C. B. Macpherson. Baltimore: Penguin Books, 1968.

————, *Man and Citizen. De Homine* translated by Charles T. Wood, T. S. K. Scott-Craig, and Bernard Gert. Edited with introduction by Bernard Gert. New York: Anchor Books, 1972.

Hofstadter, Richard, *Social Darwinism in American Thought*. Revised edition; Boston: Beacon Press, 1955.

Holmes, Jr., Oliver Wendell, *Collected Legal Papers*. New York: Harcourt, Brace and Company, 1921.

————, *The Common Law*. Boston: Little, Brown, and Company, 1881.

Horowitz, Donald, *The Courts and Social Policy*. Washington, D.C.: Brookings Institution, 1977.

Hume, David, *A Treatise of Human Nature*. Edited with introduction by L. A. Selby-Bigge. Oxford: Clarendon Press, 1973.

Hurst, James Willard, *Justice Holmes on Legal History*. New York: Macmillan Company, 1964.

Jackson, Robert H., *The Struggle for Judicial Supremacy*. New York: Vintage, [n.d.].

James, William, *The Will To Believe and Other Essays in Popular Philosophy*. New York: Dover Publications, 1956.

Jarrett, Derek, *England in the Age of Hogarth*. Frogmore, St. Albans: Paladin, 1976.

Kelly, Alfred H., and Winfred A. Harbison, *The American Constitution*. Fifth edition; New York: W. W. Norton, 1976.

Kirk, Russell, *The Conservative Mind*. Third revised edition; Chicago: Henry Regnery, 1960.

———, *The Roots of American Order*. LaSalle, IL.: Open Court, 1974.

Konefsky, Samuel J., *The Legacy of Holmes and Brandeis*. New York: Collier Books, 1961.

Kramnick, Isaac, *Bolingbroke and His Circle*. Cambridge, MA.: Harvard University Press, 1968.

Kuklick, Bruce, *The Rise of American Philosophy*. New Haven: Yale University Press, 1977.

Laslett, Peter, *The World We Have Lost*. Second edition; [n.p.]: Charles Scribner's Sons, 1973.

Letwin, Shirley, *The Pursuit of Certainty*. Cambridge: University Press, 1965.

Levy, Beryl Harold, *Our Constitution*. Port Washington, N.Y.: Kennikat Press, 1965.

Lewis, David J., and Richard L. Smith, *American Sociology and Pragmatism*. Chicago: University of Chicago Press, 1980.

Lindblom, Charles, *The Policy-Making Process*. Englewood Cliffs, N.J.: Prentice-Hall, 1968.

Lippmann, Walter, *The Public Philosophy*. New York: Mentor Books, 1956.

Locke, John, *An Essay Concerning the True Original, Extent and End of Civil Government* in Ernest Barker, editor, *Social Contract*. New York: Oxford University Press, 1962. Pp. 1–143.

———, *John Locke: Essays on the Law of Nature*. Edited with introduction by W. von Leyden. Oxford: Clarendon Press, 1965.

———, *Two Treatises of Government*. Edited with introduction by Peter Laslett. Revised edition; New York: New American Library, 1965.

Lowi, Theodore J., *The End of Liberalism*. Second edition; New York: W. W. Norton, 1979.

MacIntyre, Alasdair, *After Virtue*. Notre Dame, IN.: University of Notre Dame Press, 1981.

Macpherson, C. B., *The Political Theory of Possessive Individualism*. New York: Oxford University Press, 1962.

Madden, Edward H., *Chauncey Wright*. New York: Washington Square Press, 1964.

Mansfield, Jr., Harvey C., *Statesmanship and Party Government*. Chicago: University of Chicago Press, 1965.

Mason, Alpheus Thomas, and Richard H. Leach, *In Quest of Freedom*. Englewood Cliffs, N.J.: Prentice-Hall, 1959.

Matza, David, *Becoming Deviant*. Englewood Cliffs, N.J.: Prentice-Hall, 1969.

McCloskey, Robert G., *American Conservatism in the Age of Enterprise*. New York: Harper and Row, 1964.

McDonald, Lee C., *Western Political Theory*. New York: Harcourt, Brace and World, 1968.

Mead, George Herbert, *Mind, Self, and Society*. Edited with introduction by Charles W. Morris. Chicago: University of Chicago Press, 1962.

Mill, James, *Representative Government*. Edited with introduction by Currin Shields. Indianapolis: Bobbs-Merrill, 1955.

Mill, John Stuart, *Dissertations and Discussions*. 2 vols. New York: Haskell House Publishers, 1973.

Miller, David L., *George Herbert Mead*. Austin, TX.: University of Texas, 1973.

Moore, Edward C., *American Pragmatism*. New York: Columbia University Press, 1961.

Morris, Charles, *The Pragmatic Movement in American Philosophy*. New York: George Braziller, 1970.

Moynihan, Daniel P., *Maximum Feasible Misunderstanding*. New York: Free Press, 1970.

Niebuhr, Reinhold, *The Children of Light and the Children of Darkness*. New York: Charles Scribner's Sons, 1960.

———, *Moral Man and Immoral Society*. New York: Charles Scribner's Sons, 1960.

Passmore, John, *A Hundred Years of Philosophy*. New York: Penguin, 1966.

Peirce, C. S., *Philosophical Writings of Peirce*. Edited by Justus Buchler. New York: Dover, 1955.

Piven, Frances Fox, and Richard A. Cloward, *Poor People's Movements*. New York: Vintage Books, 1979.

———, *Regulating the Poor*. New York: Vintage Books, 1972.

Pound, Roscoe, *The Formative Era of American Law*. Boston: Little, Brown, 1938.

———, *Social Control Through Law*. [n.p.]: Anchor Books, 1968.

———, *The Spirit of the Common Law*. Boston: Beacon Press, 1963.

Robbins, Caroline, *The Eighteenth-Century Commonwealthman*. Cambridge, MA.: Harvard University Press, 1961.

Rorty, Richard, *Philosophy and the Mirror of Nature*. Princeton: Princeton University Press, 1980.

Rosenblum, Nancy L., *Bentham's Theory of the Modern State*. Cambridge, MA.: Harvard University Press, 1978.

Rucker, Darnell, *The Chicago Pragmatists*. Minneapolis: University of Minnesota Press, 1969.

Russett, Cynthia Eagle, *Darwin in America*. San Francisco: W. H. Freeman, 1976.

Sabine, George H., *A History of Political Theory*. Third edition; New York: Holt, Rinehart and Winston, 1961.

Schattschneider, E. E., *The Semi-Sovereign People*. New York: Holt, Rinehart and Winston, 1960.

Schell, Jonathan, *The Fate of the Earth*. New York: Alfred A. Knopf, 1982.

Silberman, Charles E., *Crisis in Black and White*. New York: Random House, 1964.

Spencer, Herbert, *Facts and Comments*. New York: D. Appleton and Company, 1902.

——, *Social Statics*. New York: Robert Schalkenbach Foundation, 1970.

——, *Social Statics, Abridged and Revised: Together with the Man Versus the State*. New York: D. Appleton and Company, 1896.

——, *The Study of Sociology*. New York: D. Appleton and Company, 1896.

Spragens, Thomas A., *The Politics of Motion*. Lexington, KY.: University of Kentucky Press, 1973.

Steel, Ronald, *Walter Lippmann and the American Century*. New York: Vintage Books, 1981.

Steiner, George, *In Bluebeard's Castle*. New Haven: Yale University Press, 1971.

Steintrager, James, *Bentham*. Ithaca, N.Y.: Cornell University Press, 1977.

Stephen, Leslie, *The English Utilitarians*. 3 vols. London: University of London, 1950.

Stouffer, Samuel A., *Communism, Conformity, and Civil Liberties*. New York: Doubleday, 1955.

Strauss, Leo, *Natural Right and History*. Chicago: University of Chicago Press, 1953.

Sumner, William Graham, *Essays of William Graham Sumner*. Edited by Albert Galloway Keller and Maurice R. Davie. 2 vols. New Haven: Yale University Press, 1934.

————, *Folkways*. Revised edition; Boston: Ginn and Company, 1911.

————, *What Social Classes Owe to Each Other*. Caldwell, ID.: Caxton Printers, 1974.

Thompson, E. P., *Whigs and Hunters*. New York: Pantheon Books, 1975.

Thurow, Lester C., *The Zero-Sum Society*. New York: Basic Books, 1980.

Thwing, Charles Franklin, *The American and German University*. New York: The Macmillan Company, 1928.

Tönnies, Ferdinand, *On Social Ideas and Ideologies*. Edited and translated by E. G. Jacoby. New York: Harper and Row, 1974.

Truman, David B., *The Governmental Process*. New York: Alfred A. Knopf, 1951.

Warrender, Howard, *The Political Philosophy of Hobbes*. Oxford: Clarendon Press, 1957.

White, Morton, *Social Thought in America*. Boston: Beacon Press, 1957.

Wolin, Sheldon, *Politics and Vision*. Boston: Little, Brown, 1960.

Woodward, E. L., *The Age of Reform, 1815–1870*. Vol. XIII of *The Oxford History of England*. Edited by G. N. Clark. 14 vols. Oxford: Clarendon Press, 1938.

X, Malcolm, *The Autobiography of Malcolm X*. With the assistance of Alex Haley. New York: Ballantine Books, 1965.

Shorter Works

"Attacking the Last Taboo," *Time* (April 14, 1980), p. 72.

Carter, Lief H., "Think Things Not Words," *The Journal of Politics*, XCIII (May, 1981), 315–321.

CBS Reports, "Gay Power, Gay Politics." Broadcast 10 p.m. EST, Saturday, April 26, 1980.

Cowen, Robert C., "Polluted Science at Love Canal," *The Christian Science Monitor*, June 25, 1980, p. 16.

"Cradle-to-Grave Intimacy," *Time* (September 7, 1981), p. 69.

Danford, John W., "The Problem of Language in Hobbes's Political Science," *The Journal of Politics*, XLII (February, 1980), 102–134.

Dewey, John, "The Reflex Arc Concept in Psychology," Vol. V of *The Early Works of John Dewey*. Edited by Jo Ann Boydston. 5 Vols. Carbondale, IL.: Southern Illinois University Press, 1972. Pp. 96–109.

Ernst, Dave, "Carey Backs Love Canal Study—Says Gibbs Is 'Out of Order,'" *Buffalo Evening News*, July 23, 1982, p. A-5.

Fitzhugh, George, "Sociology for the South," *Slavery Defended*. Eric L. McKitrick, editor. Englewood Cliffs, N.J.: Prentice-Hall, 1963. Pp. 34–50.

Goldman, Sheldon, "A Profile of Carter's Judicial Nominees," *Judicature*, LXII (November, 1978), 247–254.

Grayson, William J., "The Hireling and the Slave," *Slavery Defended*. Eric L. McKitrick, editor; Englewood Cliffs, N.J.: Prentice-Hall, 1963. Pp. 57–68.

Green, Barbara B., and Nancy K. Klein, "The Mentally Retarded and the Right to Vote," *Polity*, XIII (Winter, 1980), 184–206.

Havender, William R., "The Abuse of Science in Public Policy," *Journal of Contemporary Studies*, IV (Summer, 1981), 5–20.

Hershaft, Alex, "Letters to the Editor," *The Wall Street Journal*, December 30, 1982, p. 7.

Hofstadter, Richard, "The Revolution in Higher Education," *Paths of American Thought*. Arthur M. Schlesinger, Jr., and Morton White, editors; Boston: Houghton Mifflin Company, 1963. Pp. 269–290.

Liazos, Alexander, "The Poverty of Sociology of Deviance: Nuts, Sluts, and Perverts," *Social Problems*, XX (Summer, 1972), 103–120.

Loewenberg, Bert James, "Darwinism Comes to America, 1859–1900," *The Mississippi Valley Historical Review,* XXVIII (December, 1941), 339–368.

"Lois Gibbs Has Helpful Hints for Dirty Fight," *Buffalo Evening News*, March 17, 1982, p. A-3.

MacDonald, Dan, "EPA Conclusions Producing Uncertainty Among Officials," *Buffalo Evening News*, July 15, 1982, p. A-8.

Malone, Julia, "Taking Aim at Sexism Lurking Behind Words," *The Christian Science Monitor*, July 8, 1980, p. 19.

"New Power Bloc: Urban Homosexuals," *U.S. News and World Report* (June 4, 1979), p. 13.

Orren, Karen, "Standing to Sue: Interest Group Conflict in the Federal Courts," *American Political Science Review*, LXX (September, 1976), 723–741.

Rochberg-Hilton, Eugene, "The Real Relationship Between Pragmatism and Chicago Sociology," *Contemporary Sociology*, XI (March, 1982), 140–142.

Schuster, Lynda, "Livestock Lib," *The Wall Street Journal*, December 18, 1981, pp. 1, 18.

Sullivan, John L., James Piereson, and George E. Marcus, "An Alternative Conceptualization of Political Tolerance: Illusory Increases 1950s–

1970s," *American Political Science Review*, LXXIII (September, 1979), 781–794.

Vose, Clement E., "Litigation as a Form of Pressure Group Activity," *Annals of the American Academy of Political and Social Science*, CXXXIX (September, 1958), 20–31.

Wolfe, Christopher, "A Theory of U.S. Constitutional History," *The Journal of Politics*, XCIII (May, 1981), 292–316.

Court Cases

Adamson v. *California* 332 US 46 (1947).

Adkins v. *Children's Hospital* 261 US 525 (1923).

Allgeyer v. *Louisiana* 165 US 578 (1897).

Black and White Taxicab and Transfer Co. v. *Brown and Yellow Taxicab Transfer Co.* 276 US 518 (1928).

Bolling v. *Sharpe* 347 US 497 (1954).

Brown v. *Board of Education* 347 US 483 (1954).

Bunting v. *Oregon* 243 US 426 (1917).

Chicago, Milwaukee & St. Paul Railway Co. v. *Minnesota* 134 US 418 (1890).

Civil Rights Cases 109 US 3 (1883).

Eakin v. *Raub*, 12 Sergeant and Rawles 330, *Pennsylvania Reports* (1825).

Griswold v. *Connecticut* 381 US 479 (1965).

Home Building and Loan Association v. *Blaisdell* 290 US 398 (1934).

I.C.C. v. *Alabama Midland Railway Co.* 168 US 144 (1897).

I.C.C. v. *Cincinnati, New Orleans, and Texas Pacific Railway Co.* 167 US 479 (1897).

Jacobson v. *Massachusetts* 197 US 11 (1905).

Lochner v. *New York* 198 US 45 (1905).

McLaurin v. *Oklahoma State Regents* 339 US 637 (1950).

Missouri ex rel. Gaines v. *Canada* 305 US 337 (1938).

Muller v. *Oregon* 208 US 412 (1908).

Munn v. *Illinois* 94 US 113 (1877).

Plessy v. *Ferguson* 163 US 537 (1896).

Pollock v. *Farmers' Loan and Trust Co.* 157 US 429 (1895).

Pollock v. *Farmers' Loan and Trust Co.* 158 US 601 (1895).

Schechter Poultry Corp. v. *U.S.* 295 US 495 (1935).

Slaughterhouse Cases 16 Wallace 36 (1873).

Smyth v. *Ames* 169 US 466 (1898).

Sweatt v. *Painter* 339 US 629 (1950).

Turner v. *U.S.* 396 US 398 (1970).

U.S. v. *Butler* 297 US 1 (1936).

U.S. v. *E.C. Knight Co.* 156 US 1 (1895).

U.S. v. *SCRAP* 412 US 669 (1973).

West Coast Hotel v. *Parrish* 300 US 379 (1937).

Index to Proper Names and Titles

I would like to thank Pamela Lakin for her assistance in preparing this index.

Index to General Terms and Concepts